Summer of Marv

Josh Muggins

Petty Pace Press

© 2009 Josh Muggins

All rights reserved. No part of this publication may be reproduced or transmitted in any form or by any means electronic or mechanical, including photocopy, recording, or any information storage and retrieval system, without permission in writing from both the copyright owner and the publisher.

Requests for permission to make copies of any part of this work should be mailed to Permissions Department, Petty Pace Press, Minneapolis, Minnesota

ISBN: 978-1-4389-0615-7

About the Author

The patron saint of zeta males everywhere, Josh Muggins is the author of over twenty New York Times bestsellers on the culture of the Midwest in the latter half of the Twentieth Century. He is also a celebrated composer-vocalist of eleven jazz fusion albums, the creator of a popular line of salad dressings, a revered ichthyologist who designed and welded his own bathyscaphe from parts of broken-down household appliances, a silver medalist in the biathlon, an inveterate liar, and a cheapskate too tightfisted to pay a publicist to compose one puny introductory paragraph on his behalf. He can be reached at:

joshmuggins@hotmail.com

Obligatory Disclaimer

    This book is a work of fiction. Names, characters, and incidents either are the products of the author's imagination or are used fictitiously. Any resemblance to actual events, organizations, or persons, living or dead, is entirely coincidental and beyond the intent of the author—yeah, right... Thing is, I'm too lazy to do the research to justify a nonfiction label and too sniveling a coward to accept the responsibility such a label entails. Indeed, I've been known to devote up to four hours a day to nothing but sniveling.

    But I mean, really—just think about this disclaimer for a minute: *I'm* the main character in this book, so if I'm a product of the author's imagination we're risking one sumbitch of an existential paradox here, one that will inevitably suck in all the other persons portrayed in the book and ultimately you, the innocently bystanding reader.

    It's probably safer, then, space-time-continuum-wise, to consider this a lightly fictionalized memoir. There were things which I stretched, but mainly I told the truth. Expect the usual devices employed in this genre: the changing of names, the reconstruction of whole conversations from a few dimly recalled snippets, and some liberties with the chronology of events. But mostly it is a true book: with some stretchers, as I said before.

    Now if you'll excuse me, I must get back to my sniveling.

Permission

    "I'm Not in Love" Words and music by Graham Gouldman and Eric Stewart. ©1975, reproduced by permission of EMI Music Publishing Ltd., London WC2H 0QY

Admission

    I typed approximately 35 percent of this manuscript topless.

*Events in the past may be roughly divided into those
which probably never happened and those which do not matter.*
William Ralph Inge

*Some people die at twenty-five
and aren't buried until they are seventy-five.*
— Benjamin Franklin

*One man's 'growing up' is another man's
betrayal of highest principles.*
— Me, just now

*Special Introduction to the Paperback Edition**
Word on the Street is that Women Won't Like This

People ask me two questions about my work as a writer. Well, three if you want to nitpick and throw in "How can you call yourself a writer?" The others are:

Don't you spend an unhealthy amount of time living in your own past?

And:

Isn't it painful to make your younger self out to be so...so...well, so pathetic in front of literally dozens of readers?

Let me try to address both of these questions here as succinctly as possible: No.

Frankly, I like my past and have a hard time understanding people who don't like theirs. I mean, what has our past ever done to us? Has it lain in wait for us? Tortured us? Oversold us insurance? Has it maimed or killed us?

No. It's the Past's evil cousin, the Future, that's apt to do most of the above to us one day. Not the Past. The Past mostly just lies there staring up balefully at us like our superannuated family dog; it only wishes to be acknowledged from time to time and maybe have its ears scratched for an hour.

Nasty as it may have been in its fresher days, the Past isn't going to get any worse. If anything, it'll grow ever so slightly cuter over the years, as some of its characters—most notably dead uncles and teachers—take on more and

---

* All right, dammit, the *only* edition.

more flamboyance, and all the shoulda-saids and shoulda-dones inexorably morph into things actually and heroically said and done. I think you know what I mean.

That said, there is, to be sure, a two-fold problem with writing honestly about your own past: (1) You're not going to look good, and (2) the past seldom yields the sort of narrative arcs that modern entertainment consumers have been browbeaten into expecting. Searching our memories, not many of us are lucky enough to discover that we were raised in foster care only to be found decades later by our biological father, who befriended us only to dupe us into donating him a healthy kidney, thus provoking us to stalk him until he felt compelled to chuck us out an eighth-floor window, which crippled us until we fortuitously survived a jetliner crash on a remote Pacific island, where we have since found not only that we have regained full use of our legs, but that we are now imbued with a confidence and competence that has made us a natural leader and indispensable guru to our callow fellow survivors.

That, my friends, is an arc.

This book, in contrast (SPOILER ALERT! SPOILER ALERT!), traces the evolution of my nineteen-year-old self in the year 1975 from a self-absorbed, vagina-phobic dweeb to a slightly less self-absorbed, vagina-phobic dweeb. For female readers especially, I'm told, this arc is frustratingly slow and shallow, and not nearly as satisfying as, say, having a slow-moving freight train slice off young Josh's legs.[*]

If it's not too late, by the way, I would like to point out that women ought not to read this book, as it is likely to enrage them. That is what I'm told, anyway, by my test readers, two middle-aged men blessed with ex-wives and formerly teenage daughters who therefore know what it takes to enrage or mortify a female, and they're telling me that this book, with its all too frank portrayal of the nineteen-year-old male mindset, has precisely that flavor of *je ne sais quoi*.

Upon hearing this, I was not sure exactly how to respond. Personally, I'm

---

[*] This was the fate of a particularly unsympathetic male character in a movie that once held me transfixed on a transoceanic flight. I'd look up the title for you but for the fear that doing so would slow the process of erasing its existence from my memory.

not planning to stuff the Christmas stockings of my female loved ones with copies of this work, either, so I do understand my test readers' sentiment.

Still, I believe that most of the women around us *have* known a nineteen-year-old male that they cared deeply about at some point in their lives, be it a boyfriend, a brother, a son, an intern, a shirtless sweat-streaked immigrant gardener, or what have you, and so the nineteen-year-old male mindset as revealed in this book holds no untoward surprises for such worldly-wise women. They've long since cracked that code and, let's face it, former nineteen-year-old males: it's not exactly the Rosetta Stone, is it? If I were a female reader, I should think that my primary reaction to this book would be something along the lines of that warm, fuzzy feeling that comes over me whenever Wolf Blitzer graces my TV screen: an exhilarating glow of intellectual superiority. That's got to be worth a sawbuck, eh?

Look, everyone, let me just lay my cards on the table here: I wrote this book simply to try to recall what it was like to be a nineteen-year-old male in a Midwestern college town in the mid-Seventies. Because, well, that seemed like a fun thing to do…at the time. You know…plenty of jumping-off points for yarns and ruminations and cute little asides on the universality of the human experience regardless of time, place, gender, or blood-alcohol level… That's all I wanted to do… I'm really sorry. I didn't mean to wreck anything—honest.

In Mankato, Minnesota, where I spent my nineteen-year-old malehood in 1975, I believe I was reasonably happy. My baby neuroses were falling out and the adult ones had yet to grow in. Moreover, I had friends then. So you see, I just wanted to write about that bank and shoal of time, the memories of which never fail to warm the cockles of my heart. And who doesn't like warm cockles? I'm taking no guff from the cold-cockle faction this time around.

I'm serious. Death to those guys.

Josh Muggins
June 2008

1. The Good Life in Minnesota

On the eve of Super Bowl Sunday—and a Vikings Super Bowl at that—yet another Blizzard of the Century crippled southern Minnesota, the twenty-third so named storm to strike during my short residency in the state.

Undaunted, Nielsen and I found ourselves heading back to his place from our supply run around noon on game day with KTOE cranked up and the back seat of his Firebird Trans Am laden with survival rations: a case of that coveted New Ulm-brewed elixir, Hauenstein; the cheapest, foulest, most feces-shaped cigars we could find; and a copy of *Penthouse Forum* for diversion during the predestined second-half blow-out.

We were blissfully warbling along in off-key falsetto to "Loving You" when Nielsen broke the spell: "Okay, watch this!" he burbled, gunning the engine as we approached two pairs of speed bumps on the Broadmoor Apartments driveway. I braced for impact but the bumps seemed to dissolve on contact.

"Feel anything?"

"*Whooaaaaa!* How'd you do that?"

"Took me weeks after we moved in last fall to work out just the right speed that you have to hit those fuckers at."

"And that speed is?"

"Fifty-two."

I looked at him with the love that a man can only feel for another man who could land both men on a waiting list for prosthetic limbs at any moment through an errant twitch of his elbow.

Of all my chums Nielsen had changed most during my just-concluded seven-month exile from Katoland. Through much of our freshman year he had been a dorm phantom known only as "Durward's shy roommate," content to spend long days enwombed in the top bunk poring over motorhead magazines to cope with the pain of his carless existence. Once a month his girlfriend would take the Greyhound down from St. Cloud State for a conjugal visit. Thus, he was sexually prolific in a technical sense but, the girlfriend being a chubby and insecure holdover from high school, somehow it hadn't counted for much.

She was Mary—"Queen of Sots," Arnie had dubbed her—a frumpy, decidedly unregal presence most often sighted loitering outside Nielsen and Durward's room late on Sunday mornings. A sharp rap at my door would roust me from a dehydrated sleep on such occasions, whereupon I would confront a freshly laid Nielsen inviting me out for breakfast.

"Come on, Muggins! Ya *gotta* come," he would whimper. "You're the only one that can *talk* to her."

"What about Durward?"

"Turdbinder won't wake up. Might be dead."

Actually, I was no more successful at talking to Mary than anyone else, but I could at least fill dead air. So I allowed myself to be dragged along and tacked another IOU onto Nielsen's expanding account. We crunched through the snow to a fast-food place of obscure enfranchisement just off campus that offered rubbery pancake-and-sausage sets.

"What's St. Cloud like?" I asked.

"'S okay, I guess."

"A lot of drugs up there?"

"Some."

"You ever do any?"

"Couple times."

It occurred to me that these chats might constitute good training should I ever become the parent of a sullen teenager, but they were not the sort of experiential education that I craved with the aftereffects of eight beers, uncounted shots, numerous bong hits, and six white cross fogging my mind.

"Got a lot of friends up there?"

"Some."

Nielsen merrily plunged into his stack of eraser-cakes, having successfully outsourced the entire emotional-needs side of his relationship to me. He himself had taken care of the physical side the previous night on three separate occasions, so he figured he had done more than his bit.

In most instances I would have found this division of labor patently unfair, but it's hard to say how I might have responded to an offer to swap duties, sexually desperate though I was. Mary was careless of her appearance. If the phrase *low self-esteem* had been in vogue in the era, she would have been its first poster girl. Long black bangs covered her eyes, which always shifted down, left, right—anywhere but toward her interlocutor. She sagged, both bodily and in spirit, as if she had been rocketed to Earth in infancy from a smaller planet and was still struggling to cope with Earth's oppressive gravity.

During Mary's absences from the scene it was easy to forget that she existed. Nielsen certainly had no trouble doing so, segueing seamlessly into bachelorhood as soon as her bus chugged out of sight. As a free agent, though, he was no more successful than Durward or I.

I remembered thinking then, *He's about my size.*

In those days, the heights of other males seemed to fluctuate with their perceived degree of sexual experience. Arnie, for example, appeared even more diminutive than he really was because he never came remotely close to getting any.

Indeed, although I would labor mightily after his coming out to convince myself that I had always valued Arnie's unusual sensitivity, his keen aesthetic sense, his incisive views on the arts, I really just liked having a friend around who scored less often than I did—in spite of his presenting the more attractive package to the choosy female shopper. He resembled Dustin Hoffman in *The Graduate*, but with a much greater sense of self-worth. If someone had told me then that Arnie belonged to an invisible minority, I would have put my money on the Jews.

The mystery of why a fit, confident lad like Arnie never ended up with a girl was one that we, his friends, perhaps talked ourselves out of solving. He certainly wasn't shy about talking to girls; I would often eye him amusing a covey of them at a party and think, *If Arnie scores tonight and I don't, I'm putting a bullet in my head.* Little did I know then that vying with Arnie for poontang supremacy was like wearing down the Vikings in a Super Bowl: the hollowest of triumphs.

The expertise-equals-height formula had its limitations. Durward, for example, who was nearly as inept at romance as I was, would always be perceived as a big man because he so obviously was one. You tend to notice that somebody is much larger than yourself when that person is pummeling your face with his bare, meaty chest.

Nielsen, as noted, was remembered as having been my equal—around five-ten, one-forty or so—but during my absence from Mankato he had dumped Mary and acquired both a nubile nymphomaniac for his physical needs and a Trans Am for companionship, as if he were getting his midlife crisis out of the way at nineteen. And in the process he had acquired confidence and Marlboro Man good looks, with his thick black moustache and matching unibrow and permanent three-day stubble, and suddenly he seemed to stand about six-foot-two. Sexual proficiency can do that for a man: that, and jarringly fey platform shoes.

—¤—

"Oh, now what is *this* nipple-headed turdbinder trying to pull?" he moaned, as a rusty pea-green Beetle left-turned in front of us in the congested and glaciated Broadmoor parking lot, burdening him with the severe, possibly actionable strain of having to decelerate to the mid-forties.

Nielsen could be counted among those rosy souls who never saw evil intent in anyone, only rampant stupidity, which he saw in everyone in equal measure at all times. Had he been with the Forty-fifth Infantry during the liberation of Dachau, his gut reaction would have been "Oh, what has that dumb fuckwad Hitler been up to *now*?" before pausing to mutter, "Cracklicking retarded Austro-Hungarian dingbat…"

"Is Jimbo going to be there for the game?" I asked, referring to the semierect primate that Nielsen had dragged up from Meldom that year to share rent. "And his girlfriend? What's her name?"

"Midge!" he barked, as if trying to dislodge a stubborn lump of mucus from deep in his gullet. "Fuck, no. She'll drag him off somewhere. That no-mind piece of shit is so whipped. He brings her over twice a week and they fuck for three minutes, and that's all I ever hear of them these days."

Jimbo can go for three minutes? I thought but dared not say.

"I hope you don't mind if I say that I don't care much for Midge."

"Fuckin' moron is what she is," said Nielsen. The affirmation was superfluous, but I was grateful for it nonetheless. He was always thoughtful that way.

As Nielsen had predicted, the emissions of our cigars soon drove away Midge with a bleating Jimbo in tow just before kickoff.

"It's still early," we said ritualistically throughout the first half, but those brave words would roll thickly off the tongue—*izz stillerly*—as the game and the case of Hauensteins dragged on. Broadcasters began resorting to the old "taut defensive struggle" chestnut by the third quarter; we weren't buying any of that. Nielsen had flipped open the *Forum* and was already regaling me with his formidable oral-interpretation skills. "'My engorged member,'" he read. "Ha-ha. *Engorged*. That's good. That's a good word." He was relaying the denouement of a tender interlude between a lonely protagonist and his freshly delivered cheese pizza when some obscure Viking from special teams valiantly flopped down upon a blocked punt in the Steelers' end zone to spare us the shame of a shutout. The point after was wide, however, and the unimpressed Steelers quickly made up the touchdown.

Final score: 16-6.

Unofficial battle cry of the Bud Grant-era Vikings: *Z'dillerly*.

—¤—

I tend to say *we* when referring to Minnesotans, but in this as in so many other aspects of my adult life I am a fraud, a charlatan, a poseur. Let's stick with *poseur*. I like saying that.

Josh Muggins

I grew up in western Illinois, an area noted for nothing.* For some reason, I began to pine for Minnesota in my high school years. Perhaps this was because Bob Dylan sprang from that mythic land, or perhaps because its government had recently decriminalized marijuana. But more likely my longing stemmed from the fact that Minnesota was one of those few states that had a distinct identity, which Illinois clearly lacked. We didn't even have a personal proper noun, for heaven's sake. What *were* we? Illinoisites? Illinoids? Whatever our ethnicity, I was a self-loathing one-of-those.

Minnesotans, in contrast, knew exactly who they were. Minnesotans were the nation's second fiddles; its silver medalists; the bridesmaids but never the bride; the tireless strivers who always fell just short of making it all the way. And to someone with my track record with girls, sports, grades, mustache-growth, what have you—well, second-fiddlehood seemed a thing devoutly to be wished.

Falling Just Short could have been the state motto in those years, when we (there I go again) kept churning out fizzy politicians who never quite made it to the White House and sports franchises that brought out the best in the ultimate victors of countless League Championship Series and Super Bowls. Our preeminent boxer, Duane Bobick, is best remembered for charitably raising the spirits of true champions both Olympian and professional. But surely the most iconic Minnesotan of the period was The Very Capable Kenny Jay.

To The Very Capable Kenny Jay, that doughy sacrificial lamb of the American Wrestling Association, Falling Just Short was more than a pastime: it was a way of life. By 1975 he was roughly halfway through a losing streak of some six hundred fifty consecutive televised wrestling matches, along the way authoring a résumé bespattered with the sweat and saliva of many an AWA Hall of Famer. He had been bolo-punched by The Crusher, drop-kicked by Vern Gagne, whipped into innumerable turnbuckles by Nick Bockwinkle, ardently masticated upon by Mad Dog Vachon, pounced on from the top

---

* This despite my quixotic campaign to see it legally designated "the Bermuda Triangle of Dubious Presidential Birthplaces." Starting from my hometown, Mortonville, and heading out west, east, or north, one can reach the boyhood homes of Herbert Hoover, Ronald Reagan, and Ulysses S. Grant respectively in little over an hour. Few are impressed.

rope by Handsome Harley Race—*even though that's banned in some states and should be in this one!*—tomahawked by Wahoo McDaniel, clawed by Baron von Raschke, poleaxed by Ivan Putski, and tummy-tickled into submission by Pampero Firpo, the Wild Bull of the Pampas. There were career prostitutes near Medicare age who had spent less time on their backs flailing in feigned emotion than the Very Capable Kenny Jay had.*

At seventeen I begged to be allowed to apply to Mankato State College even though I had never visited the campus, and my perplexed parents finally caved. In August 1973, a month before I would depart, *Time* ran a cover story titled "The Good Life in Minnesota," thereby acknowledging the providential wisdom of my choice.

On its cover the strapping young governor, Wendell Anderson, held up some sort of monstrous fish that he had apparently just yanked bare-handed out of one of those Ten Thousand Lakes I'd been hearing of. He sported a plaid flannel shirt and a squinty grin that suggested he had been taking advantage of some newly decriminalized substance or other and that, as soon as the camera crew left him alone, he was going to chomp into that still-twitching invertebrate with the ravenous zeal of Mad Dog Vachon tucking into a full course of The Very Capable Kenny Jay.

People called him Wendy. The governor was "Wendy." "Pennies fer Wendy!" cashiers would chirp when tacking state tax onto a lunch check. In Illinois, our governors were known by their penitentiary numbers, or they died dubious deaths with shoeboxes full of large-denomination bills in their bedroom closets.

In September 1973 we crossed the state line on US 218 in Dad's '70 Ford Torino, a.k.a. the Republicanmobile, and cruised past a town called Lyle. Even the towns sounded friendly. "You Are Now Entering Minnesota, Drive Safely," said Lyle. *Hi, Lyle. I'm Josh.* I knew I was home at last. It was like

---

* The VCKJ's career would reach a little-known apex the following year when he was pummeled into submission by Muhammad Ali himself—an honor that eluded even Duane Bobick. As always, his role was to help promote the Upcoming Event, in this case a closed-circuit TV spectacle involving the boxer and Japanese wrestler Antonio Inoki. It was Kenny's lot in life to be the sizzle, never the steak—a distinction no doubt lost on Mad Dog Vachon.

geographic-reassignment surgery. All those years, I had been a Minnesotan trapped in the body of an Illinoiser. Illinian. Whatever.

But after less than nine months in Mankato, I had been forced into exile: a summer job in Illinois followed by Fall Quarter abroad in dreary old London. Thus, with 1975 a'borning I was nineteen years old and had yet to spend a full year in my true native state, and that needed to change. For as much as I liked to say *poseur*, I had no ambition to remain one.

2. Meanwhile, Back in Ingrid's Vagina

It was a dark and stormy night in Ingrid's vagina.

Eight months after my first—my only—foray there, nothing had changed. Nothing. One could almost believe that the thing had just lain there dormant all that time—but was it in any way reasonable to suppose that? Ingrid was not exactly Penelope, nor I Odysseus returning from the Trojan War. Ingrid was on birth control as usual, so no Trojans of any sort were involved here.

It seemed a perfectly fine vagina as such things go. Not that I had any basis for making comparative judgments, of course, but it seemed that all my brother members of the species *Mankatus erectus* did, and those silver-backed chaps were always eager to go on at length about the myriad vaginas they had encountered, whether encouraged to do so or not. Anyway, all the characteristics touted by those vagina connoisseurs—moisture, warmth, good hygiene (at least vis-à-vis my own), and attachment to the body of a lithe and enthusiastic young woman—were present and accounted for in Ingrid's case, so I felt confident in declaring it a perfectly fine vagina.

Still, I wished that Ingrid's vagina would simmer down a bit. Excursions into the thing were like space walks, brief by definition and yet fraught with peril. It still broke into a savage pistoning as soon as penetrated, as if some internal security device had been triggered to repel the intruding entity. Or perhaps the nonstop undulation was intended to gratify the vagina itself and/or the intruder. I could only speculate, as there was no reasoning with the thing.

Whatever its cause, all this commotion was draining and terrifying. The only part of me that did not remain rigid throughout the procedure was the item that was supposed to. When mechanical bulls became a popular fixture in bars later in the decade, I would think *that's probably a lot like Ingrid's vagina* while watching braver men flail around on them. In either case, the rare man who could last a full minute before ending up on the floor in a heap of quivering protoplasm could call himself a winner. Or so I told myself.

I contemplated just asking Ingrid about it: if anyone had ever lasted a whole minute, that is. I'd read somewhere that distracting oneself from the task at hand was a good way to stave off a premature finale, and the one thing that could be said with certainty about conversation with Ingrid was that it distracted. And no time like the present for said distraction: that telltale rumbling to the south signified that this bull-ride was rapidly nearing an abrupt and messy end.

But any attempt at idle chitchat between Ingrid and me would be futile. We had reconfirmed that fact earlier in the evening at Haley's place.

—¤—

Haley's soiree at his house on North Fifth had ostensibly been my welcome back party from Fall Quarter abroad in London, though it was safe to assume that the group would have found an alternative excuse to sauté some extraneous brain cells that night without me.

I had cruised back into Mankato the previous afternoon–greeted again on Route 14 by the twenty-foot Happy Chef, still grinning defiantly against a gray and featureless January sky, still brandishing his colossal spoon, still standing silent sentinel over his eponymous roadside diner—with a three-point agenda: to get a job, to achieve local fame as a writer, and to penetrate a vagina, preferably human. Now, here I was crossing one goal off the list my second night back; and the other two would fall by the end of the month. Mankato in 1975 was the land where dreams came true.

Oddly enough, Haley had beaten me to the punch on the literary fame front.

"Some freak came to interview us about substandard housing for students," he told me. "He was from that newspaper."

"The *Reporter*?"

"No, that other thing. That magazine. *Juggs*?"

"Oh, *The Medicine Jug*."

In his kitchen, Haley offered Miller High Life in a bottle and a gray, saliva-drenched pin-joint. His deep-set eyes looked like bowling ball holes in the piercing glare of the flickering fluorescent bulb.

"I guess. He was going around talking to everybody who rents from our landlord, the son of a bitch."

"The guy who interviewed you was a son of a bitch?"

"No, our landlord. Anyway, the freak took a bunch of pictures and made us show him all the shit that's wrong with the house."

"And they published it? That's tits, Haley."

His long, stringy, dark hair made him look like a buff, sedate cousin of Tiny Tim. He drove an agglomeration of rust that in a former life had been a Fairlane and he enjoyed genital intercourse regularly and effortlessly. I envied but could not hate him.

"Hey—you wanna see something weird?"

"Uh-huh."

Haley produced a golf ball, and the first question to strike me was how on earth we were going to smoke it. Instead, he demonstrated that the ball, placed in any corner, inexorably wound a course to the center of the living room. It was a phenomenon that induced a parched and awed *Whooaaaaa!* from every first-time guest and I was no exception; but then again we were all great *Whooaaaaa!*ers in that era and would *Whooaaaaa!* quite literally at the drop of a hat since, after all, gentlemen didn't wear hats in those days so when someone showed up in one, that, too, was worth a *Whooaaaaa!*

The living room floor itself was quite *Whooaaaaa!*-worthy indeed—more like a tightly strung trampoline than flooring. Sometimes it was hard to tell where the suggestibility brought on by drugs and alcohol left off and physical reality began, but not this time. The floor definitely gave a bit when one walked across it. The orange, faux-Indian tapestry that Haley employed as a rug twisted when a toe was dipped into the middle of it, mimicking a textbook illustration of a black hole.

That the living room was deserted in the middle of a party had not surprised me, since Haley had *The James Gang Rides Again* playing at top volume in there. Some things never changed. But now, having inspected the floor, I attributed everyone's abandoning the living room to simple self-preservation.

It was, however, an off-season outbreak of Chest Boxing in the front yard that had drawn away the crowd. Nielsen and Durward, the lads from Meldom—the cradle of Chest Boxing—were about to square off for their sixty-fifth rematch.[*]

Once Nielsen was dispatched, I elected to brave the subzero elements and challenge Durward myself. I was unfazed by his sixty-pound advantage, as I had never seen a Chest Boxing match whose outcome had hinged on sheer size—or agility or strategy for that matter. Rather, it was the combatant able to hold out the guise of taking the whole enterprise seriously for a longer time who invariably triumphed. I was fairly good at this and so had felled other plus-sized foes, but in Durward I was facing the world's first bona fide Chest Boxing Hall of Famer: the Pasha of the Pecs, the Rajah of the Ribcage. The Nabob of the Nipples. The mere sight of his rubbery, hairless farm-boy frame galumphing toward me as he bounded—nimbly for a lad of his girth—from toe to toe across the tundra of Haley's yard, supplemented by his Tarzan-like ululations of attack, had me on my knees before he made his first lunge. I was no more a match for Durward's heaving chest than I would be for Ingrid's heaving vagina later on.

The agony of defeat notwithstanding, I was glad to have had an outdoor respite after all of Haley's refreshments. Such was the magic of the Minnesota winter: it sobered one up so that one could start afresh at whatever quest one

---

[*] For the uninitiated: Practitioners of the lost art of Chest Boxing stripped to the waist and tried to pound each other senseless using only their chests. Imagine the congratulatory chest-bumps exchanged by athletes of a later era, only with murderous intent. Shoulder-rolls were regarded as fouls and head-butting was right out. One simply got up a good head of steam and rammed one's opponent chest-on. The sport's brilliance lay in its simplicity.

Summer of Marv

wished to embark upon, which more often than not was to repeat the cycle. After all, if you're in Mankato and it's January, you're not exactly swimming in entertainment options. However, Ingrid and Co. had arrived at the party in the meantime, and from the moment I laid bloodshot eyes on her it became inevitable that I would drive her home.

Nine months had passed since my last encounter with Ingrid and her vagina without so much as a postcard to either of them, and so it should have amazed me that she was ready to be driven home that night, and yet it didn't, and that's how I ended up back in the darn thing again.

—◻—

So now I found myself tripling my lifetime sexual experience with a whopping 1.5 minutes in the inferno and then...

"*Whooaaaaa!*" I said, with double intent, only to be doubly ignored.

So there they went, another battalion of top-gun sperm, wriggling deep into the sweltering depths from whose borne no wriggler returns—some two hundred and eighty million of them. That was a lot of sperm in 1975; worth close to four hundred million today. Nearly half a billion, Canadian. *Vaya con dios, amigos.*

As I lay in the darkness of Ingrid's bedroom with my benumbed arm under her, I might have asked myself, *Just who is this Ingrid? Why is she so nice to me?*, but I didn't, in large part because I was an asshole, in my own naïve way no less despicable than the more worldly vagina-obsessed yahoos who were my friends and classmates. So I figured that I knew all I needed to know about this person who always seemed to come along for the ride whenever her vagina showed up.

Ingrid had first materialized amid a covey of C-wing girls at one of our McElroy E-wing Wednesday night keggers during freshman year. What unfolded thereafter neatly paralleled one of those comic book story lines in which, say, the Justice League of America is besieged by a pack of super-villains who, as luck would have it, each possess a power that makes him a perfect match for one-on-one combat with a particular Leaguer. *Batman, this is Owl-Man. Owl-Man? Batman.*

Thus our resident heart-throb Lex quickly zeroed in on the similarly poised and dexterous Bonnie, soon after which mellow Haley paired off with woozy hippie-chick Margaux. Next came the mutual gravitational attraction of Durward and the Rubenesque Joan.[*] Finally, Ingrid and I stood alone, the last two scrawny ten-year-olds forlornly kicking the dirt along the foul line, still unpicked.

In sharp contrast to her vagina, Ingrid herself was shy and unthreatening. She wore plain white tees, no makeup; kept her black hair shorter than mine and never styled. Her stringy body was toned from workouts with the women's track and field squad, for which she ran middle distances and occasional sprints. To the then ascendant notion that participation in sports affords young women greater self-esteem and cooler judgment in choosing sex partners, she was the exception that proved the rule.

Her eyes drooped at the corners, suggesting a sadness contradicted by her winsome smile—features which reminded one of nothing so much as that gigantic Happy Chef statue at the edge of town, a resemblance scarcely conducive to amorous exploit. When alarmed, her voice warbled like a turkey's—or rather, like a third grader badly playing a turkey in a Thanksgiving pageant—and she was always alarmed. At first I thought it was my fault but later noticed that she talked that way to everybody.

How we finally ended up in bed remains a mystery lost in a fog of beer and speed. I suppose we both felt that by not doing it we were letting down our respective teams. The only sentiment I remember her sharing with me on that first occasion was "You're so *sweaty*."

I offered to use a condom then, even showed it to her: the new-fangled ribbed kind touted for functioning like thousands of tiny fingertips urging a woman to let go. Alas, she wasn't buying it. I was sure the desensitizing layer would add precious nanoseconds to my playing time. If only there were

---

[*] "She had torpedo tits," Durward had famously said afterward, not deliberately being ungallant but simply desperate to supply the sort of evocative detail that would bolster his case during a tough post-coital murder board. We had left him alone in his room with Joan only two minutes earlier and thus found it suspicious to encounter him fully dressed and Joanless. His efforts at verisimilitude, replete with disconcertingly Old MacDonaldesque sound effects, eventually swayed the jury to validate his status as a nonvirgin despite its refusal to accept the freshly used condom into evidence.

some legitimate grounds on which to overrule her—say, some deadly and horrifying form of venereal disease that necessitated protection during such casual encounters—but then again, if pigs had wings...

I emerged from my room to thunderous applause from my African-American neighbor and his friends as they savored toilet-paper-core-sized joints across the hall. The ovation was premature; I merely wanted to shower off the offensive beer-sweat. Not until morning was the deed finally done.

I would never come to think of her as my girlfriend, nor would I perceive any desire on her part to be so regarded. A later generation might have termed us Friends with Benefits, but in fact the friendship was just as awkward as the benefits.

The morning after Haley's party, I prepared to flee Ingrid's apartment feeling pretty pleased with myself. After all, less than a week into 1975 I was one-for-six in Nights Scoring. Then again, a lot of obscure middle infielders are batting way over their heads at a comparably early stage in the season. Career stats tell all, and mine still made me out to be the Moonlight Graham of sex.

Muggins, Joshua L.
Born: Oct. 22, 1955   Bends: Right   Dangles: Left

Year	League	TO	TOWP	NP	Ave	MP	MOG	MOR	OOG	OOR	GOG	GOR	Slg.
1967	Hetero	47	0	0	.000	0	0	0	0	0	0	0	.000
1968	Hetero	155	0	0	.000	0	0	0	0	0	0	0	.000
1969	Hetero	282	0	0	.000	0	0	0	0	0	0	0	.000
1970	Hetero	311	0	0	.000	0	0	0	0	0	0	0	.000
1971	Hetero	348	0	0	.000	0	0	0	0	0	0	0	.000
1972	Hetero	391	0	0	.000	0	0	0	0	0	0	0	.000
1973	Hetero	377	0	0	.000	0	0	0	0	0	0	0	.000
1974	Hetero	384	1	1	.003	0.7	0	0	0*	0	1		.000
1975	Hetero	5	1	0	.200	1.5	0	0	0	0	1		.000
Tot		2300	2	1	.001	2.2	0	0	0	0	2		.000

Key: TO = Total Orgasms TOWP = Total Orgasms With Partner NP = New Partners Ave.= TOWP/TO MP = Minutes of Penetration MOG = Manual Orgasms Given MOR = Manual Orgasms Received OOG = Oral Orgasms Given OOR = Oral Orgasms Received GOG = Genital Orgasms Given GOR = Genital Orgasms Received Slg.= Slugging Percentage (Total Orgasms Given / Total Orgasms Received)

Josh Muggins

* During his quarter abroad in London, Muggins recorded one OOR outside Heterosexual League play. And people wonder why he writes under an assumed name.

Ergo, my continuing dependence on Ingrid: the only pitcher I could hit.

Upon leaving her apartment I said, "I'm not very good at this."

"It's okay," she gobbled softly.

The matter of phone numbers did not come up.

3. Another Mankato Depot Tragedy

The Mankato depot and its environs fairly reek of ghosts chained to the tracks by unhappy events of the town's formative days. U.S. Grant's disgraced ex-Vice President keeled over there in the midst of a speaking tour on ethics in government; less ironically, the largest legally sanctioned mass execution in American history likewise took place in the vicinity. Just ghosts all over the place. One couldn't chuck a Frisbee around there without slicing through three or four ectoplasms.

Thus, it was not a place where anyone would choose to spend a long overcast midwinter night. But as with all dirty jobs, someone's gotta do it, and at around two-thirty during one such dark, somber vigil, a luckless railroad employee rubbed his eyes and sipped his cold coffee under the sickly fluorescent lights of his austere depot office. No freights were scheduled to pass through soon so the sight of any vehicle gliding into view would have struck said employee with no small degree of alarm. A deadheading locomotive, say, would have been disturbing enough; a Dodge Challenger thumping along the railroad ties with a besotted college sophomore at the wheel was quite off the scale.

What he did not seem to realize at that moment was my equal degree of disorientation at seeing a railroad employee peering at me, his fingertips and nose pressed flush against the windowpane, his face a pinkish mask of terror.

The pinkish mask of terror vanished from the windowpane and, after an interval that was probably less than a minute but seemed much longer, rematerialized outside the window of my car. "Yer drivin' on the *railroad tracks!*" he informed me.

"Yes. Yes, sir," I said. "I rather thought I was."

"You...you drove about a *hunnert yards,*" he added, as spittle congealed into lovely silver globules on the bristles of his brown moustache and quivered there, solidifying, "down my goddam *tracks!*"

There was a story that went with my driving approximately a hunnert yards down those very goddam railroad tracks which this man seemed to hold in an odd proprietary esteem, and so I scanned his face, searching for a glimmer of willingness on his part to serve as an audience. Judging from his age, I supposed that he had been pulling the midnight shift at the depot for upwards of ten years. His duties, I imagined, were simple enough: to signal a few scattered freights as they rumbled through town, and to keep the tracks clear of besotted sophomores.

On the latter point at least he had performed with unfailing vigilance lo these many years and plainly did not take kindly to having his immaculate record besmirched. Thus I spared him my story, as it was a long one, sensing that the removal from his railroad tracks of my Dodge Challenger, a.k.a. the Mortonville Missile, was higher on his list of priorities than finding out how it had gotten there in the first place.

Had he lent a more willing ear, I would have informed him that I had just finished escorting Jan Kelso safely home. Jan Kelso! Queen of our quarter-abroad cohort! A shimmering shaft of radiant warmth cast forth by God to pierce the dense, murky vapors of London in late autumn.

A prim Catholic princess and "little sister" for an especially pompous fraternity, Jan clearly had little in common with the likes of Ingrid. Middle-distance running was not for Jan, let alone sprinting. Jan did not sweat. Most forms of excreting and secreting were surely beneath her.

What I had failed to appreciate was that Jan had even less in common with the likes of me, and—more relevant to my pursuit of her—regarded me with condescending bemusement. Fortunately, I was then, as now, genetically immune to condescending bemusement: the stuff rolls right off me. But I soon came to realize that new, more elaborate seduction tactics than those which I usually employed (i.e. trolling parties for females drunker and less discriminating than myself) would be required in this case, the odds of randomly finding any particular female drunk and undiscriminating at a party—Jan Kelso especially—being depressingly low.

So I decided to give this "dating" concept I'd heard tell of a whirl by offering to chauffeur her to a reunion gathering of our London group. It was at this party that I intended to render her drunk and undiscriminating, but instead only succeeded in doing so to myself. It wasn't hard, as I had the "undiscriminating" part down pat from the get-go.

It was well after midnight when, amid heavy snowfall, I got Jan back to her North Mankato hilltop palace. I received a closed lip kiss (three seconds), which I accepted as the most a bong-breathed suitor could hope for on a first date, followed by the same condescending guffaw with which she had greeted me at her front door so many hours and beers earlier.

By the time I had made it back to the Belgrade Avenue Bridge, the streets were deserted and, owing to the snow, invisible. In normal conditions it would have been a piece of cake: cruise smoothly to the right off Belgrade onto Riverfront Drive, then take a left onto Warren. But now there were no tire tracks to follow—only a calm ocean of fresh snow, all of a uniform hue, depth, and texture, stretching from Riverfront to Siberia. Adding to the intricacy of the task were the traces of Jan Kelso's lipstick that lingered on my mouth and the molecules of Kelsovian perfume that dusted the complex stitching of my nasal hairs.

Owing to these factors, the fantasy film originally slated for screening in the privacy of my room a half hour later—in which the secretionless goodnight kiss led to a soggier kiss and thence to a feverish embrace and thence to an escalating series of events culminating in a three-towel secretion smashup—had begun to unspool in my mind of its own accord. Surely anyone could see how even the most alert and experienced driver might turn a little too soon and end up jouncing merrily down the railway ties instead of veering onto Riverfront Drive. Under the circumstances, just keeping both hands on the wheel constituted an admirable display of restraint.

The walrus-faced depot official would have none of this—no, nothing of Jan Kelso or of nasal hairs caked with perfume molecules. A practical man, he was back inside working his way down the listings of service stations to see who could send a tow truck.

"Jesus Christ, you drove a hunnert yards down the goddam railroad tracks!" said the leader of the two-man towing team, showcasing those keen powers of observation common to all working-class Mankatoans.

"There's an interesting story behind this," I assured him.

"Oh, man, I don't even know if we can get you off. We'd better call the cops on this one."

There ensued an impromptu negotiation for which I was ill-prepared, starting at a hunnert dollars and culminating with the inquiry "Well how much you got, then?" I had lost my capacity for duplicity several drinks and one goodnight kiss earlier, so I told him I had sixty, and he took all of it, and there went my drug budget for the rest of the winter.

—◻—

Whatever pheromones of my own I may have deposited on Jan Kelso's nasal hairs failed to find purchase there. With twenty-twenty hindsight I can see that my chances of ever seducing Jan were worse than those of a drunken frat boy hitting the swimming pool from a fifth-floor Cancun hotel room. But the sting of this failure was offset somewhat by a successful interview with the *Reporter* editor early the following week.

My weekly column would not bring in enough money to make up for the Depot Debacle, though, nor did my night dishwashing job at the Yum Yum Inn suffice. I was thereby forced into the term paper writing business to raise drug funds.

I put an ad in the *Reporter* and had a dozen clients within a week, including one Jan Kelso. In lieu of payment, she took me out for dinner and drinks. Presumably she wanted to show me how this dating business properly worked prior to giving me up for Lent, but the lesson didn't seem to take.

Another client named Wanda similarly wanted to make payment in drinks and was also nominally female. She boasted a dirty-blond mullet and rippling musculature that foreshadowed the action movie heroes of the following decade. Her habitat: the South Street Saloon, more specifically the game room there, where she insisted that I join her in liberating the foosball table from the naugahyded pair of frat boys that had laid claim to it.

"We kicked their *asses!*" she crowed, reddening my palm more radiantly than a triple feature of Jan Kelso fantasies with a vicious high-five. Mental note: Never challenge Wanda at Chest Boxing.

Several beers later we were on the bed back at the dorm exchanging tongue-borne bacteria cultures. I was about to make a break for second base when she excused herself. A restroom visit was inevitable after all that beer, I reasoned, so I waited. And waited. And waited. Visa processing in Casablanca took less time than this. I might have begun to think that she had run off on me except for the fact that this was her room.

I began to do what came naturally when I was a guest in such situations, i.e., to read that person's mail. I couldn't find much: only a postcard from her grandmother, reminding her that she could be really pretty if she would just apply makeup a little more judiciously and smile more often.

I wrote her a note of my own and headed back to McElroy Center. It was Valentine's Day, 1975.[*]

—◻—

But February did not slide away without further success. Ingrid graciously invited me back into her vagina to shoot a sequel to January's episode, which had left so many unanswered questions. It was not to be a feature-length work or even a decent short. Barely a trailer, in fact. After a mere sixty-two seconds, hundreds of thousands lay dead or dying in yet another sperm Antietam.

This was getting old, ending up this way after a long night spent successfully overleaping the countless obstacles to getting a woman in bed, conscious and

---

[*] As readers of the CliffsNotes version know, Wanda makes this single brief appearance in the book to symbolize knowledge and morality in an increasingly bestial world. No, wait: that's Piggy.

naked and willing. It was like those annoying games of solitaire when you finally get all the cards turned over and yet somehow still can't win.

    I blamed Jan Kelso for my poor performance. It was the involuntary, split-second transposing of her face over Ingrid's that had immediately preceded the ill-fated Charge of the Sperm Brigade. Then again, I was blaming Jan Kelso for everything that went wrong in my life in those days, still blaming her, in fact, for the sixty dollars squandered at the depot, which, I would soon discover, could have purchased a sixpack of spiffy professional handjobs at the Sauna Inn.

4. Just That Stupid

"You guys," said Arnie, firing up the first joint of the morning, "aren't ears just the *grossest* things?"

"Your ears or mine?" I asked mid-toke.

"No, just *ears*. Like, *everybody's* ears."

While the joint wound its way to the back seat I tried to study the nearest available ear—Arnie's left—without taking my eyes off Route 14. These days one never took anything for granted while at the wheel. Even on a clear April morning with sparse traffic and a wide-open prairie vista ahead, a renegade set of railroad tracks could spring panther-like out of nowhere to ensnare one's vehicle.

"I never really thought about it before," I conceded. "But now that you mention it, they *are* kind of…crinkly."

"I mean," he said, "imagine you were an alien and you landed here and saw humans for the first time. Wouldn't you think, 'My God, look at the *ears* on these things! Why don't they *keep them covered up?*' I mean, can you *think* of a tackier looking body part?"

Though intended as a rhetorical question,[*] it soon had everyone lost in

---

[*] Other issues raised by Arnie on similar occasions included Isn't it great that we were all born white speakers of English?, Aren't dogs better people than people?, Why isn't Liberace properly appreciated by our generation?, Wouldn't it be neat if people aged in the other direction?, and Why isn't tap water blue? He also put forward a remarkably prescient editorial on the likelihood that human activity could accelerate the melting of polar ice caps—in 1974, mind you—and vowed to do his part to save the world by remaining immobile in his dorm room for four days so as to reduce human-motion-caused "friction in the atmosphere."

wordless, hazy thought.

"Cats' ears are nice, though," purred a backseat passenger as she slowly exhaled a hit.

—¤—

An hour or so later, upon coming to my senses, such as they were, I was most pleased to see the round canopy of my military surplus parachute fully deployed above me, all strings attached. The only sounds at three thousand feet were the gentle rustling of said canopy in the wind and someone insanely cackling, who, by process of elimination, would have to be me. From above, the fading whir of a small plane could be heard intermittently.

A dozen blurry seconds earlier, I had stepped onto the wheel of the plane and pushed off at Cap'n Dave's command. Now I saw that the static line had performed its function admirably, freeing me from the unlikely chore of opening the reserve chute…and I was wafting.

And it was *go-o-o-od*. Good wafting, I assumed, was even harder to come by than genital intercourse, and certainly seemed to last longer. The last time I had wafted as carefree as this, amniotic fluid had been my medium. Sometimes there was an updraft! *Wheeeee!* Updrafts were good: they prolonged the ride. If a pollster had wafted past at that moment, he or she could have put me down as staunchly pro-updraft.

There was a vague sense of neglecting some errand but I couldn't guess what it might be. And did it really matter? Could anything matter besides this Etch-a-Sketch-sharp view of miles and miles of patchwork farmland? Could *anything* matter but this exquisite moment, this ultimate rush?

As I wafted farther down, microbes skittering around the runway became distinguishable as Arnie, Cindi, Freddie, and Cap'n Dave's assistant. My three classmates had completed their dives on the Cessna's first flight of the morning, but as they constituted a capacity load I had volunteered to be the child left behind, thus risking the chance that higher winds might cancel a later flight. That had been big of me, I had told myself.

Now they were waving at me. I returned the gesture. *Hi, there! Now I know what you were cackling about when you hit the dirt!*

Summer of Marv

They were not cackling now. They were yelling.

Soon, their gestures and shouts took on some coherence. It was Arnie's voice that pierced the welkin first: *"You're not steering it right!"*

It was then that I noticed the bright orange roof of the hangar wafting up to meet me. I was being drawn to it as if it were a huge refrigerator and I a scruffy little sophomore-shaped magnet. The original plan called for wafting three thousand feet from the plane to an X painted in the dirt, to which the other three novices had all come damnably close. On my current trajectory I was fated to waft twenty-nine hundred feet from the plane to the roof of the hangar, where I would roll snugly into my chute and plummet the rest of the way, neatly shrink-wrapped for burial.

"Pull the strings!" Arnie implored. *"You're not doin' it right!"*

—¤—

It was Arnie's idea in the first place, of course. It was Arnie's idea that we sign up for the noncredit skydiving course, Arnie's idea that we stick with it even after the first two long drives to the Rochester airfield had proved fruitless due to high winds, and Arnie's idea that I be the designated driver for the group. "You're car is *so* tits, Muggins," he had purred. "The lines! And the *color!* If I were your car, I'd dump you."

After I had been extracted from the mushy soybean field into which I eventually plopped, after I had suffered Cap'n Dave's rebuke for muddying my military surplus chute ("Just how hard is it to hit an *airfield?*"), we found ourselves on our way back to Katoland, the aroma of Arnie's gourmet weed filling the Missile and the Pabst Blue Ribbon flowing freely. Windows long sealed were at last cranked open as the flat farmland rolled by and the sweet soil-scented wind washed over us. Spring was announcing its return engagement in Minnesota this Saturday afternoon and we were feeling it in our every atom.

Frat-boy Freddie, a tertiary character,[*] printed wedding invitations at

---

[*] There is a curious phenomenon that I have noticed through memoir writing: Tertiary characters have an astonishing and universal tendency to mistake themselves for primary characters when encountered in the flesh. It's enough to make one posit the existence of some parallel universe in which the Freddies of this world are the puppet-masters and *we* the tertiary extras. But only after far too much weed.

Pearlman Printing. Cindi, now riding shotgun, had been unknown to us before the course. A lissome and laconic grad student with close-cropped black hair, she lived alone in an upscale apartment complex off Glenwood Avenue.

"You guys, you know—if we, like, *died* right now, it would be all right," Arnie chortled, sinking into the back seat and smiling his squinty smile, as he was wont to do in moments of stoned triumph. We toasted that notion.

Outside Owatonna, Cindi asked, "So what are you guys doing tonight after we get back?"

The three of us responded that our immediate plans centered on contacting as many friends as possible in order to describe our successful jumps and gloat. We took the idea and ran with it, competing: I'm going to go hit all the bars and tell everybody I ever met. Oh yeah? Well, I know a guy in the band that's playing at the Gurdy, so I'll get him to announce it to *the whole bar*. That's nothing: I have anchorman Chuck Pasek's home phone number, so you just wait and see the Channel 12 news tonight.

Near Waseca, Cindi, whose flannel shirt was one button more open than it had been a beer earlier, said, "Maybe I'll go out tonight, too… Or maybe I'll just stay home and make dinner. By myself. You know, just have a quiet dinner for myself…at home."

Someone said that was cool and made a motion, quickly seconded, for another joint.

Around Janesville, as things grew foggier, Cindi might have said, "Yes, that's what I'll do. Just stay home and eat dinner by myself. Stark naked," to no avail; and by Madison Lake she may as well have screamed, "Goddammit, I'm an attractive, highly articulate young woman so jazzed from my virgin skydive that I'm practically throwing myself at a carload of dorks, and *you guys can't take the hint?* What's the story here? Are you all gay? Or really just that *stupid?*"

To which, if alert enough, we would have replied:
"Just that stupid."
"Gay."
"Just that stupid."

That would have been Arnie in the middle there, though we wouldn't find out that he was gay until the Eighties, by which time he had gravitated to the West Coast. Then again, Freddie and I did not come to grips with the fact that we were just that stupid until around the same time. We're all in one closet or another when we're nineteen.

But it had been raw craft on my part to say that I would hit the bars that night, for I had other, more nefarious plans in mind altogether.

—¤—

Around midnight, I fired up the sleek-lined, forest-green Missile and headed downtown.

Then again, not exactly downtown: it was to that obscure area west of downtown off South Front, where Park Lane crawls up under the huge shadow of the 169 overpass, where good things of day begin to droop and drowse while night's black agents to their preys do rouse—yes, yes, *that* was where I pointed the Missile.

At a pink-neon-trimmed establishment called the Sauna Inn, a jolly, earthy woman in her forties named Angela took my massage and sauna fee (ten dollars), led me to my locker and thence to the sauna. She told me that Rita would be ready for me soon. This came as welcome reassurance that my massage would come at the hands of a non-Angela life form.

The sauna itself was a narrow, woody crypt, but I had it all to myself along with its bountiful library of steam-soaked magazines: *Oui* and *Gent* and other august bulwarks of the genre. I was peeling apart the inner layers of a vintage *Dude* when the door opened and a human tide of mottled flesh rolled in, howdying me a boisterous howdy.

"Not too busy here tonight I guess," noted the new arrival, causing me to wonder, with no little awe, what it would feel like on a more typical evening to be saunaing with a half dozen Wild Turkey-scented clients of comparable mass.

"'Fraid I shouldna had them last two-er three shots," he hooted, pawing a soggy *Adam*. "Better check me out one of these. Ya don't wanna go out there all limp, ya know."

I nodded, limply.

"Nothin' worse than payin' yer money and then just floppin' around out there—'m I right?"

I smiled, all the while inwardly screaming *Shut up with the impotence riff already!* There ought to be some sort of law against broaching that subject in a massage parlor, like the injunction on making bomb jokes while passing through airport security. There is simply no room for First Amendment absolutism in a sauna joint, not when one is ten dollars deep in a dubious sexual investment.

Then, as if to punctuate his point, his large bowel unleashed a long and rippling expulsion, evocative of two soggy decks of cards being shuffled together by a clumsy blackjack dealer. The Lord works in mysterious ways, and I was convinced that this mottled minion of the damned had been sent to thwart my sinful scheme. First he had stifled my inspiration; now my respiration.

The sparse furnishings in the main room of the Sauna Inn appeared to have been left behind by the building's previous tenant: the Mengele Dental Clinic, perhaps. My day had begun under an Army surplus parachute and now was ending on a hospital's surplus gurney.

The stabs at establishing an amorous ambience were half-hearted at best. Sheets of translucent pastel fabric had been slung from the ceiling to mute the severe lighting. Somewhere tinny Muzak wheezed from a dying radio. Rita appeared, and briskly pulled flimsy vinyl curtains along squeaky ceiling-mounted runners to conceal us inside a semi-private cocoon.

For the moment the rest of the room was empty, but soon enough Mr. Limpidity himself, Flopalong Cassidy, would make his presence felt again. I could only hope that I would be done with my business before he appeared; but this wish merely fanned the flames of my raging performance anxiety.

"Oil or powder?" asked Rita. She was a college-age girl and yet plainly not in college. Her yellow short-sleeve blouse was tight but not revealing; her straight brown hair carefully combed; her makeup subdued. Her appearance made her seem suited for waiting tables in a Front Street diner, as did her overall attitude toward work, a tone of practiced and artificial friendliness. She struck me as the kind of girl who received helpful notes from her grandmother explaining that she could meet a really nice boy if she would just smile more often.

I opted for oil.

"Okay. I need you to roll over on your stom— *Keep the towel on!*"

"Sorry!"

"'S all right. Just house rules is all. In case the cops come in… Okay, just relax."

To review: a loud, foul, cud-chewing client was certain to ramble into the room soon. The Mankato Police Department might also crash the party. I was out ten dollars, and even a brief accidental exposure of my private parts could induce a shriek of panic. Relax…

Soon warm, slimy oil was slathered on my shoulders and neck and back. Rivulets of the substance trickled off me on both sides like soapy residue running off the Missile's roof at a carwash.

"You're tense," she observed as she worked my shoulders.

"Um, well, I jumped out of an airplane today."

"Huh?"

"I mean, I went skydiving."

"Cool. Where?"

"Near Rochester."

"Oh… You do that a lot?"

"No. It was my first time. Probably my last, too."

"How come?"

"I don't know. It's just one of those things you do one time, so you can say that you did it… You know what I mean?"

"You can roll over now."

Could I? Both the gurney and I were so lubed up that I could gain no traction. Keeping the towel in place added another degree of difficulty to the maneuver. I twisted spastically and finally lay stiff and slack-jawed on my back, like a freshly landed walleye atop a frozen lake.

Soon my chest, arms, and right leg were drenched in oil. Had someone given me the Heimlich maneuver at that point, my entire ribcage might have squirted out of my slimy carcass through a shaving cut on my Adam's apple. Not a pretty sight.

I began to ask her about her hobbies, interests, hometown. Though my goal in doing so was to fill dead air, she seemed grateful for the attention. It was while her hands were winding a greasy path up my left leg that I found myself inquiring as to the chances of getting some, as it were, extra service.

She looked me in the eye for the first time and then turned away.

"We're not supposed to do anything. The cops have been coming around."

I had no parry for that. "I'd really appreciate it. Anything at all. Anything?"

A pause, then a dry whisper: "For ten bucks, I can use my hand."

These were the most erotic words that had ever been addressed to me. I liked handjobs—in theory, at least. There was something familiar, safe, elemental about the act. That the handjob, that quintessence of carnal minimalism, had been so widely relegated to foreplay was, I felt strongly, an injustice on a par with forcing Rick Derringer to open for Edgar Winter. No slight against Edgar intended—after all, in this analogy he corresponds to genital intercourse, and I suspect he could live with that. The point being simply that the handjob in those days needed a new agent.

I tried to ease myself out of the swamp of goop.

"Where you going?"

"My wallet. It's in the locker."

"Pay me later," she hissed. "Just call it a tip."

She removed the towel to reveal my vast, crinkly limpness, which seemed to address Arnie's earlier question re body parts more disturbing than the human ear. She winced at the sight for a second until her professionalism reasserted itself and that diner-waitress smile returned.

There was silence now throughout the Sauna Inn but for "Rock Your Baby" on the screechy radio and the melancholy squishing of Rita's slippery fist pumping away. The cruel reality that hand-penile negotiations had deadlocked became harder to ignore with every passing squish.

"Could I, uh, see you?"

"No, man. I can't take my clothes off."

"It'd really move things along. Believe me, it would."

There was a squishy pause.

"You can open my shirt."

I did, and the impact on our progress was immediate. Her bra cups reminded me of twin parachute canopies, which I strongly associated with both safety and pleasant wafting. She would not unhook the garment but allowed me to explore its contents. This action drove my thoughts toward Cindi, or more specifically toward the glimpse of cleavage Cindi had offered while easing herself out of the Missile that afternoon. That broke the stalemate; Rita's hand ran with it, pumping with newfound zeal.

Within a minute I was thanking Rita, thanking her, Elvis-like, very, very much, and she smiled at me for the first time, and her hypothetical grandmother was right, she could look fetching when she smiled with feeling.

Later, as I was slipping Rita her honorarium, I had an epiphany re Cindi's comments en route from Rochester. It dawned on me that instead of paying twenty dollars for the privilege of conjuring up Cindi in the place of a dour masseuse, I could have spent this time with the real-life Cindi. And probably for nothing more than the cost of a mediocre bottle of wine. And probably could have gotten more than just a handjob out of the deal…perhaps even— dare I dream such lofty dreams?— *two* handjobs. And I certainly could have evaded Angela, the soggy library, Flopalong Cassidy, and all that oil.

That was a day that, as it drew to a close, I rather wished I could have done over. Then again, I pretty much felt that way at the end of every day in Mankato in 1975. At the end of every week, month, and year, for that matter.

I began to wonder more and more what it might feel like to attain physical gratification in the presence of a woman while thinking about that very same woman. I had a gnawing suspicion that it would feel most agreeable. And I had another, more aggressively gnawing suspicion that I would never, ever find out.

31

5. One Night on Front Street

"I'm going to be a regular columnist for the *Reporter*," I announced the next night at Mettler's.

"Tits," muttered Nielsen.

It was not immediately clear whether he was acknowledging my news or providing commentary on the live entertainment, as a portly, undulating performer on stage had just exposed those very organs, much to the delight of the mostly working-class spectators. They were long and tubular,[*] evocative of plummeting warheads or, viewed from a different angle, spent torpedoes, and thus they summoned up recollections of Durward's estranged deflowerer, Joan.

It was perhaps for this reason that Durward unleashed on that performer a stream of imperative statements too vile to be printed even here, and yet somehow poetical in their rhythm and alliteration. But later that night, Durward's muse would be silenced when we returned to our base of operations two doors down Front Street, the fabled Rathskeller, and ran into none other than the original Joan along with Ingrid *et al* on a girls' night out.

It turned out to be Ingrid's birthday. I gave her a bottle of Miller right away and other fluids in private later on. In between, I danced with her. As much as I would like to claim authorship to this impulse, it was in fact the glares of her friends Margaux and Bonnie that sealed the deal. Even a

---

[*] The organs, not the spectators.

liquored-up dolt could decode the unspoken message *You'd better get out there and dance with our friend on her birthday if you expect to retain the privilege of having incompetent sex with her* in those four icy eyes.

I outfoxed the lot of them, though, by dancing even more incompetently than I sexed: running in place, biting my lower lip, and miming a series of one-armed chin-ups. It really was the best I could do, and I couldn't tell if Ingrid appreciated it or not, but the effort helped assuage the guilt I was feeling for neglecting her between sojourns into her vagina these several weeks. Greater love hath no man than to dance at the Rat's with City Mouse on stage.

During a post-fifth-beer respite, Arnie challenged me at pinball while Nielsen offered encouragement.

"Think Durward will get back together with Joan?" I asked, peeking into the ballroom to confirm that Ingrid had not been poached.

"Nah," said Nielsen. "That concubine is so fuckin' stuck up now. She goes with some turdbinder from Devonshire."

"A concubine," Arnie added, "to the core."

I was on the brink of an epoch-making pinball comeback when the mournful cry *Last call for alcohol!* sliced through the hallowed air of the Rat's, and I headed back to the ballroom to face my destiny.

At her apartment Ingrid gobbled nonstop for twenty minutes and then unleashed the vagina on me again.

While I was developing a tepid affection of sorts for Ingrid herself, this vagina of hers was another matter entirely. Most small, furry creatures can be subdued by the full weight of an adult human male, but not this thing, pound for pound as ferocious as a wolverine. Somehow, I toughed it out.

When I came to in the morning, I realized that I was now averaging a whopping 1.5 Genital Orgasms Received per month on the year, but still needed to work on getting my minutes up. At some submerged level I was beginning to suspect that the problem lay in the way I regarded not just Ingrid, but women in general.

It wasn't as though I looked down on women—certainly not by the standards of Mankato males of the era, at least. It was I, after all, who had plucked the relatively dignified, Latinate *concubine* from *Roget's Thesaurus* and force-fed it into our communal lexicon after wearying of the constant drumbeat of *slut, skank,* and *whore.* ("*Concubine*—I *like* it," Nielsen had enthused.) Not much as feminist credentials go, to be sure, but more than any of my peers could lay claim to.

I viewed women in 1975 exactly the way I viewed Jack Nicholson then: with unmitigated awe at all the things they were capable of doing and a fervent desire to see them do those things more often. The analogy wasn't perfect, though, for I at least had the courage to approach women when both they and I were drunk whereas, in a similar scenario with Nicholson, I certainly would have demurred.*

I prided myself on what I liked to characterize as my daring disregard for social convention, for meaningless formalities, for "going through the motions" in the course of building a relationship. I was still the better part of a decade away from figuring out that most women actually *like* the motions and formalities. But that's neither here nor there. At some level I knew even then that I would have to get over this Nicholson Barrier with females.

It occurred to me briefly, in light of recent circumstances, that I might get more playing time if I declared myself a free agent and signed a contract outside the Hetero League.

---

* The following winter, Tertiary Freddie, the heterosexual skydiver, claimed to have done very nearly that when he found himself waiting in line behind Jack when checking into a Vail ski lodge. The exchange reportedly went as follows:
Tertiary Freddie: Hi, Jack.
Jack Nicholson: *Huh?*
 I envy him that encounter to this day.

6. Meanwhile, Back at the Yum Yum

The front door of the Yum Yum Inn safely bolted, Johnny was free yet again to confide to me via the Wurlitzer that he had shot that man in Reno for no purpose—none—other than to watch him die, and like so many other listeners I took the lying rascal at his word.

Around two a.m., Paul, the pallid one-man sanitation crew, would join the party, would stack up the chrome-legged chairs with their torn, fire-engine upholstery and shove the square laminated tables with their wobbly cross-foot bases against the wall to improve his access to the spilled crumbs of butterbrown potatoes and bits of burger garnish and splotches of condiments that dotted the faded gray linoleum. Then he would drag his mop around the room, rearranging the grime into Pollockesque swirls. I dared to ask him once—since we had the place to ourselves—if he created his art deliberately, and he replied "No," flicking a booger with practiced aplomb into a wastebasket behind the counter to signal a stern refusal to explicate his creative process. Paul was a Renaissance Man if ever Mankato spawned one.

It was then, in the last hour of my shift, that I so often heard Johnny's confession: long after closing, after the departure of all the blister-faced patrons and of Jimmy, the spherical Lebanese owner.[*] I could play what I

---

[*] All small businesses in Mankato in 1975 were operated by squat, florid Lebanese-Americans. It may have been a civic ordinance. The mayor himself, owner of a corner grocery store, was a squat, florid Lebanese-American. So was the proprietor-chef of the only Japanese restaurant in town.

35

wanted on the juke box—usually Neil Young or Johnny—to cleanse the palate of selections like "Mandy" that Jimmy played to soothe the savage beasts, while reading the *Free Press* at my leisure. If Paul had any objections to my jukebox ritual, he characteristically kept his own counsel.

"I hear a train a-comin'," Johnny averred in that old familiar warble.

—◻—

When I had taken on the night dishwashing position at the Yum Yum the very idea of shooting a man just to watch him die—in Reno or anywhere else—would have struck me as highly eccentric, even uncouth, but that was before I met Red, one of our late-night regulars.

Red, a lazily nicknamed orange-haired behemoth, was forever trying to embroil me in a business scheme that involved a small investment on his part in exchange for my kissing his ass. I had been sweeping up the remains of a Coke glass he had knocked to the floor one night in February when the issue first arose, the inspiration apparently being the momentary proximity of my lips to his buttocks as I stooped to scoop up the shards. "Hey kid," he had bellowed, "while yer down there, I'll give ya a quarter tuh kiss muh ass!" The coin in question glinted before my eyes between the calluses of thick digits dripping butterbrown potato grease. I respectfully declined.

Despite the disappointingly soft smattering of laughter from his fellow patrons, Red, a fellow of most finite jest, would reiterate his offer numerous times during those bleak winter nights, sometimes sweetening the pot to a full dollar. I still wasn't biting; Red's rear was as wide as the Minnesota River at some points in its winding course and far less self-cleansing. Then, perhaps owing to the recession that so bedeviled the nation that winter, he suddenly bartered me down to a mere twenty cents for full-fledged oral gratification before I knew what was what.

In many ways, Red epitomized our rednecky clientele. The Yum Yum sopped up the overflow crowd from the Happy Chef and other classier diners along the Madison strip. Men on the way home from the Bodega or the Caledonia, drunken and gastronomically undiscriminating working-class men—the culinary equivalent of overstimulated girls who might actually make out with me at a party—were our regulars.

I thus spent much of my Yum Yum tenure wondering whether the abuse from Red and his ilk was worth the dollar-eighty an hour that Jimmy paid me in a small brown envelope each week, well below the federal minimum wage that had recently rocketed to a dizzying two-ten. I was a man with responsibilities, after all: by this time I had a daily amphetamine addiction to feed along with an ongoing binge drinking habit. Not unlike having two kids and a mortgage, to my mindset.

On the plus side, Jimmy did have the good grace to leave every night around one o'clock, thus affording me the opportunity to loot his walk-in coolers on my way home.

Around three, I would wearily load the iced-over Missile with whole tenderloins and chickens and assorted seafood, would scrape a thin rectangle of the windshield free of frost and, peering through this slit the way a jousting knight might peer through the visor of his helmet, would plunge down Madison toward Haley's house—where he and his housemate Barry had hauled their refrigerator out to the garage—and dump the contraband.

That Haley had a handy midnight dumping site for purloined loins was providential, as he alone among our band of brothers could manipulate fire to render foodstuffs palatable—mouth-watering, even. Every Sunday we would gather at his slowly collapsing shack for an orgy of bacon-wrapped filet mignon, baked chicken, jumbo shrimp, beer, weed, and perhaps strawberry mescaline for dessert. Haley, dreamy-eyed and unflappable in his general outlook on life, was fussy in his kitchen. "Next time, steal more bacon," he would grouse now and again. But my Yum Yum days were already numbered.

—◻—

One thing about the Yum Yum that I knew I would miss, even as I gave Jimmy notice, was its aura of mystery. Going by the name alone some MSC acquaintances assumed I was working in an opium den that sidelined in white slavery.

That cachet frayed, however, as curious ethnotourists began trekking from the dorms to ogle me in my nocturnal habitat. One night, Spook Blunt dragged Thurman Lee along with him in some sort of stoned, misguided bid to integrate the Yum Yum. To their credit, the clientele proved color blind: "Well, lookie there," one awestruck redneck giddily inquired of another. "Is that there feller *black?*"

Red was not in attendance that night but was growing ever more truculent by that time, citing my long, wavy black hair and even my Fu Manchu as evidence of esoteric sexual proclivities. One night he accused me of being a "hat shitter," a charge to which I could not even imagine the proper reaction.

The final blow came just a few nights after that, when tiny pinkish orbs of light appeared through the Missile's frost-caked rear windshield as I was en route to deposit plunder with a plate value of two hundred dollars into Haley's fridge. My sheepish bleats of contrition induced one of Mankato's Finest to let me off with a final warning to scrape my windows properly, which I took to heart, and soon I left professional dishwashing (and food piracy) for an exciting new career in napkin printing.

7. An Exciting New Career in Napkin Printing

"You're *that guy*, arncha?" I heard someone snarl behind me one day in April, soon after taking refuge from the Yum Yum at Pearlman Printing. I braked my napkin printing press and turned to face some sort of rabid Scotsman in a tank top and cut-off jeans, a gangly figure, all sewn together from shocks of orange hair and long, angular hairy limbs, with a bushy, pubic-red mustache and zits and a Paleolithic jaw. "Aren't you that guy? That *Reporter* guy?"

I admitted warily that I was, indeed, that guy.

"Oh, hey! Well…" he said, his tone still as high and piercing as some fierce bird of prey's even as his demeanor softened. "Just wanted to say that I like your stuff. Well, except that last column. I didn't really get that one."

I thanked him. There was an awkward pause, during which he seemed to wait for me to deconstruct that recent column so that he could belatedly slap his remarkably hairy knees and guffaw over its theretofore impenetrable hilarity. When I didn't, he flapped his arms and stalked back to his press, red-faced.

His name was Cary. I had heard my new supervisor, Marv, greet him as such during our tour of the plant earlier in the week. Now I felt badly about brushing him off. He was just trying to be friendly, I supposed, and had no way of knowing how wary I had grown by then of the *You're that guy!* opening gambit.

I tried to finish my order of two hundred monogrammed silver-on-pastel-green cocktail napkins for Lee Ann and Cletus of Myrtle Creek, Oregon while puzzling out how to make things right with this Cary character. Just then Marv hove into view, waddling down the aisle between the rows of hotstamp presses.

There was something of the antique Roman about Marv. It was in the hair to an extent, a style that fell somewhere between a Durward-esque farmboy bowl-cut and the stately patrician bangs adorning a thousand glassy-eyed marble busts in a thousand museums. (Marv's bangs were black and ever so slightly curled.)

It was in the attitude: superficially jovial and avuncular and yet apart, for a department head ought not to get too cozy with the rank-and-file.

It was in the frame, to be sure: six-foot-two with a posture that could be described as either "ramrod straight" or "corncob up butt" depending on one's dialect. He seemed a fine figger of a man, though it was hard to determine exactly what sort of figger lurked under his loose-fitting shop-coat.

It was probably that shop-coat most of all, the way it hung about him like a long black toga. When he strode into the break room, one expected the assembled plebeians to rise and greet him in unison with a hearty *Hail Marv!* and then draw their daggers and carve him as a dish fit for the gods.

Marv began effecting repairs on the press facing mine. With his back to me, he applied a hacksaw to a horizontal bar on the machine while its female operator looked on with that crinkle-browed expression of awe and concern that women often adopt when an authority figure is bringing large, dangerous tools to bear upon a machine or child or other possession that they value. Marv gripped the hacksaw at pelvis level, where, from my perspective, his toga-coat obscured it from view.

This gave me the opportunity I hoped for; I found Cary two presses down the row and summoned him back to my work area just as Marv began to make brisk upward-angled thrusts with the saw, lurching backward and forward with increasing vigor, and though it became unnecessary to point out what Marv appeared to be doing, Cary and I could not resist copiously doing so anyway, delighting each other with obscure colloquialisms for the

Summer of Marv

deed.* At the sound of our giggles Marv paused to cast a self-conscious glance over his shoulder before resuming his zestful thrusting, and in such moments unbreakable bonds of comradeship are forged.

—◘—

It was Tertiary Freddie who had encouraged me to seek employment at Pearlman's on the day of our skydives. Marv and I found Freddie in the Invitations Department on the morning on my orientation tour of the plant, a blue aluminum-sided structure off 169 toward St. Peter.

Pearlman's masters had concluded—and not without reason, if one took the Yum Yum clientele into consideration—that a part-time workforce consisting mainly of college students would prove more spirited and less prone to labor agitation than the usual blue-collar crowd. Thus, it wasn't surprising to discover throughout the plant an abundance of familiar flora and fauna, both fratty and freaky. For MSC students, pulling a half-day shift at Pearlman's before or after class was almost as cliché as pulling a dorm fire alarm in a spasm of midweek boredom.

"Oh, not only napkins. Not by a long shot, no sir!" said Marv on that occasion, dispelling a misunderstanding that I had not had. "The invitations, the matchboxes, the coasters—the whole wedding shebang! Look, I've gotta make my rounds, but we've put together this manual for you—"

"Just for me?"

"Well, no—for all the new hires. It'll let you see what we're all about here. Chad'll be around if you have questions."

And so he left me there at his desk on a wooden platform, overlooking his domain. The manual that he had recommended explained that we printed two types of napkins, luncheon and beverage, both of which were "available in a colorful assortment of," well, "colors." Most orders were for weddings but some were to commemorate other assorted tragedies. Customers from all over the United States visited their local representative to scrutinize the samples and select a design, which would appear above the names of the doomed duo and

---

* I was partial in those days to "Looks like Marv's strummin' on his ol' banjo."

their date with destiny. There was a sample pasted into the manual which showed intertwining flowery vines encircling the phrase…

…And the TWO shall become ONE

…and beneath it:

Betty Jo and Trevor
March 19, 1974

The manual went on to describe safety tips for operating a printing press, but it failed to grip the reader. It lacked character development, depth. The mind kept rushing back to these Betty Jo and Trevor. Who were they? And *where* were they? And what had moved them to take this unthinkable, cataclysmic step on March nineteenth of last year? Whatever had become of them? Had Betty Jo, like the praying mantis, devoured Trevor soon after a successful mating?

I gave up on the poorly plotted manual. Besides, the method of operating a napkin printing press was on full display in front of me and therefore needed no elucidation in prose.

Two rows of eight hotstamp presses faced each other, each press walled off from its neighbor by a high wooden work-bench painted a bright canary yellow. The press jaws rocked open and shut as the operator laid blank napkins one by one onto a pad.

And so, all aglow beneath a broad skylight, the napkin printers printed merrily on, the whir and whomp of machinery providing rhythm for the harmony of their cheery chatter, the spent streams of gold and silver foil spilling from the backs of their machines and writhing like glistening snakes in the no-man's land between the rows.

And all of these press operators were zany college kids like me! Half of them female! Would one of my coworkers offer me a quarter to kiss her ass? Unlikely, I supposed, but one could dream.

Like Romulus before me I had had enough of life among the wolves and yearned to be with my own kind again. In Marv, I had already found my Caesar. Would that in Pearlman Printing I could find my Rome.

8. Men Dare Call Him Spook

Our Writing and Reading the News for Television instructor was on a roll, his twin beetle-brows curling toward each other as though threatening to meet, and mate, then and there on his forehead, his burnt-orange corduroy suit—garish even for the Seventies—spewing its sinister light rays deep into our defenseless retinas.

His theme: the airy-fairy new phraseology that, abetted by sloppy broadcast journalism, was insidiously corroding national discourse: expressions like "his or her," "pro-choice," "Native American" and such. He seemed all the more frustrated by the nonexistence of a convenient garbage-pail term—"political correctness," say—into which all such lexical sewage might be shoveled.

"Just take this term *inner city*, for example," he sputtered. "I mean, *inner city!* What the hell is *that* supposed to mean?"

He did not expect nor wait for class participation.

"*I'll* tell you what it means. *Niggers!* That's what it means!" And for those who missed the thrust of his argument the first time around, he shrugged and summarized: "*Niggers!*"

Two frat boys—wannabe Dandy Don Merediths—nodded and giggled in the back of the room. This was going to be a fun term for them. Most of the faces had gone as blank as they were white. Spook Blunt, possibly the whitest man in the long and checkered history of Caucasitude, folded his arms across his chest, lowered his head and, to the extent that congenital necklessness permitted, sadly shook it, his body language proclaiming *I'm seriously thinking of reporting this to the dean.* One man alone among those present was sending our instructor the negative feedback he so clearly deserved and it was not me: it was the man men dared called Spook.

The instructor, a real-live broadcast journalist from the Cities, deflected Spook's eye-daggers using the supra-spectral powers of his suit, but would retaliate some weeks later when we all took our turns reading copy in front of a camera at a faux news desk, after which we collectively viewed the film.

"*Posture!*" barked our mentor the moment the image of Spook hunched over the news desk burst onto the pull-down screen. "Look at that *neck*, those *shoulders!*" he cawed, thrashing Spook's ghostly visage with a wooden pointer. "You're too *tense! (Rap!)* Too *wound up! (Rap!)* And those *eyes! (Rap!)* The camera's not going to *bite* you, son! You look like you're on the verge of *panic!*"

No, no, no, I yearned to interject. You don't understand. He can't help it. That's the way he looks *all the time.* He looks that way when he's *asleep,* for heaven's sake. For I had seen it.

—▫—

Alas, poor Spook: I knew him. Fickle Fate and the gnomes in the housing office had conspired to settle him in the room across the hall from Nielsen and Durward our freshman year.

Finding in Durward Roe a fellow farm boy from a neighboring county, Spook assumed that they would quickly forge strong bonds, but neglected to inform Durward in advance of this unilateral stealth-bonding. Durward might be strolling downstairs toward the cafeteria while bouncing some free verse off Nielsen and, suddenly sensing that he had acquired an entourage, turn to find Spook bobbing along at his heels, at which sight he would, from time to time, let loose an involuntary yelp, and that was how Stan Blunt became *Spook*.

There was something vaguely martial about him in a toy soldier way. His blond, tangled, Brillo-pad hair angled upward like a built-in salute, and he walked with a stiff and solemn gait, as though forever softly marching in a funeral cortege. His neck being so stumpy, he tended to pivot at the hips when casting a glance to one side, a physical quirk that Durward mimicked with merciless precision. He shaved his pubic-hued sideburns into perfect trapezoids and wore oval glasses with thin silver frames, all of which made him look like a much scaled-down version of somebody's dad; and in fact he was, at twenty, notably older than other freshmen but could not possibly have been anybody's dad, since the *in vitro* procedure had yet to become commonplace and he was clearly a virgin.

Most of us were virgins when we started our freshman year, of course. Like SAT scores or the universal lust for Marcia on *The Brady Bunch*, it was one of those topics not broached in polite society. We were virgins in denial. In this present, more enlightened but more intrusive age, I suppose someone would stage an intervention and force the likes of us into Virgins Anonymous.

Even though virginity was not uncommon, Spook somehow managed to be even more flamboyantly virginal than the rest of us, perhaps just because he'd been at it longer. He was allowed conditional admission into our group owing to his ownership of a car and willingness to drive us to liquor stores. As the year wore on, however, his silent dogging of our heels grew wearisome and he would have to pay dues for his continued access to our companionship in the form of a campaign of terror.

In its most common form, terror came by way of untimely blackouts. He might be lying rigidly on his bed with a textbook cracked open on his pelvis, smoking a Marlboro and listening to the favorite of his four records (*Ain't no sunshine when she's gone… Bum…bum…bum…*) when the breaker switch for his room would mysteriously shut down, forcing him to march down the hall to the utility room, where Durward would pounce upon him from behind the door, wailing a war-cry of indeterminate ethnicity and dressed, for reasons perhaps only his Maker could discern, in his tae kwon do robe and a Fred Flintstone mask—the latter accoutrement being especially superfluous, since Durward's face *au naturel* resembled nothing so much as the face of a Bedrock quarry intern.

With a curt hip-swivel, Spook finally turned his back on us and bestowed his society on those residents of the floor who would surely sympathize with his persecution, the African American cohort. Now he could be glimpsed from time to time amid the contraband smog in Thurman Lee's room across the hall from mine.

I feel more at home here. I belong with these guys, I can feel it, he would tell himself whenever a prolifically Afroed linebacker from Miami passed him a joint the size of a flaming rolled-up *Reporter*, and indeed his new associates accepted him with a collective shrug and even introduced him to LSD, albeit without the usual courtesy of telling him that they were doing so. After eight distressing hours staring at the ceiling above his bed and wondering why his roommate seemed to be floating there reading *Moby Dick* in a long-dead Middle Eastern tongue, Spook accepted his destiny and returned to our fold, despite redoubled harassment. The incident no doubt scarred him for life though it was hard to tell with Spook, who always gave the impression that life itself had scarred him for life.

By our sophomore year we knew we were not going to be rid of him. He wisely moved over to McElroy's F-wing, which established just the right degree of separation. Seeing less of him now, we began to appreciate his finer points, of which there were many. For one thing, he made it clear—the Acid Incident notwithstanding—that he would not tolerate racist wisecracks from his peers any more than he would from some vile, self-centered nimrod who thought he was doing us a favor by driving down from the Cities to teach our Writing and Reading the News class. Courtliness and a natural concern for others ought to be added to the list, too, for these are virtues that one finds all too rarely in post-college life, making them more precious than they ought to be but admirable all the same.

—◘—

Apart from the journalism course with Spook Blunt, memories of my final two quarters of academic life are fuzzy. All I can dredge up about Introduction to Poetry, for example, is the crabby white-haired dean of the English Department who attempted to teach it, and her propensity for drilling us unremittingly on distinctions among the terms *metaphor, simile* and so forth.

An uncomfortable silence ensued one day when she asked the class to define *synecdoche*. Finally, someone managed to explain that it was a literary device by which the writer used a part of something to signify the whole of that thing, or vice versa. Unsatisfied, she pressed for an example, perhaps hoping against hope that someone would regurgitate a recently assigned poem in which "ten sail" signified ten ships. I raised my hand and came very near suggesting "Like using *vagina* to mean an entire woman?" before I managed to stop myself, and soon thereafter dropped the course for my own safety.

I also took a Wolfgang Fendrich class that term—the name of which I wish I could say is forgotten but in fact was probably never learned to begin with—with Arnie, Nielsen and Durward: Wolfgang devotees all. A Wolfgang Fendrich class in 1975 was the closest a Mankatoan could come to the thrill of catching the Beatles singing "Hey Jude" on a random London rooftop, so widely beloved were the esoteric pieces of performance art that Wolfgang called "classes."

It was fun to identify freshmen new to the Wolfgang experience because they looked so profoundly uncomfortable when he did his shtick, scanning the circulated attendance clipboards and wondering aloud why Mona Lott never answered when called upon, or lamenting the recently sagging attendance of the once rock-solid Hugh G. Rection.

"You think Wolfgang will do his rant on the hypocrisy of grades again?" burbled Arnie. "That would be just *so* tits."

"Fuckin' Wolfgang," mused Nielsen, with an endearing lilt that he had never been known to use for foreigners.[*]

Occasionally Wolfgang would yield the stage for the bulk of the hour to members of the class who opted to do a presentation, for which one's grade got bumped up to an A. (Under Wolfgang's popular grading scheme even the likes of Dick Getzard could pull a B just for regular attendance.) Such days were fraught with the potential for a let-down, rather like staying up for *The Tonight Show* only to hear the dreaded words, "…and sitting in for Johnny

---

[*] Wolfgang's exact roots were unknown and his accent hard to pin down, but he was rumored to be a Holocaust survivor. When I met him once in the sauna—the one in the field house on campus, not the gamier one downtown—I thought I detected a numerical tattoo on his forearm.

tonight: *John Davidson!*" And yet these guest hosts—mostly foreign students itching to even centuries-old scores before a mystified rural Minnesotan audience—could be engaging in their own right at times.

"We are not *Arabs!*" the Iranians would shriek, choosing to leave undisputed the *Commie* and *asshole* segments of the epithets being tossed at them by frat boys in the back while simultaneously provoking their simmering Arab classmates to sue for equal time.

I, for one, had not been aware that Iranians were ethnically distinct from Arabs until that day, nor had I theretofore encountered the pseudonym Pat Magroin, and these two morsels of knowledge, impossible to disentangle, would one day constitute more than I retained from any other college gen-ed course.

And yet that's not entirely true, because I certainly associate vivid memories with Health and Hygiene.

The genial lesbian in charge of that class insisted that we learn hygiene experientially, and offered a handy list of ways to earn points through activities on and off campus.

Perhaps the least appetizing item on the menu was a visit to a dental hygiene clinic in the basement of Morris Hall, but that's the very one I went with. As my family had long been blessed with good dental genes, I figured to be in and out in ten minutes with a signature on my achievement card.

The basement of Morris Hall, however, gave me pause. Though the whole campus was only a few decades old, a time portal seemed to whisk one into a medieval era at some point along the descent to the musty subterranean level of Morris. Sclerotic lamps flickered purplishly overhead. The thick rusty door to the clinic yielded with a low, grudging groan.

The Frankensteinian decor extended to the interior, which was cavernous and dank. But spread throughout this broad chamber were several cones of vivid halogen light. Each cone illuminated a dental hygiene chair and a future dental hygienist, every one a lithe female in a mint-green dental hygienist pantsuit. There was the bloodcurdling impression that all of them had been standing there, utterly motionless, until the moment the door had creaked open, bringing them to life and cuing them to unfurl their radiant dental hygienist smiles full-force upon me: the Stepford Dentists.

The cleaning and counseling procedure took thirty minutes but seemed to flash by in two. The most engaging part, unlikely enough, was the flossing demonstration. So intense was my hygienist's concentration as she squeegeed my every incisor that it overrode her anti-ogling radar, thus affording me a leisurely, guilt-free tour of the gently rolling scenery within her loose hygienist top. And when she went all the way back to floss the molars—ah, the *molars!*—there was the actual pummeling of the side of my face with swaying hygienic boobs. This was Chest Boxing at its most refined.

One left the dental hygiene clinic in such a blistering state of high hygiene that one could hardly wait to get back to one's dorm room and lock the door. And yet, somehow it slipped one's mind to share this improbable discovery with male friends. One never spoke of the dental hygiene clinic. It was rather like Fight Club that way.

So I would easily pass Health and Hygiene and the nameless Wolfgang class, but nothing else, and thus had clinched a spot on the academic probation list for Spring Quarter. No worries there, though, since I had already resolved to drop out of school.

—◻—

Ingrid had vowed to appear at the last of our weekly jumpstart-the-weekend keggers on the last Wednesday in May, thus freeing me from the burden of providing my own relief after a particularly vigorous farewell flossing. By eleven that night it was back-in-the-saddle-again time, Ingrid's-vagina-wise. By eleven-oh-two it was out-of-the-saddle- again time, and Ingrid was weeping.

I assumed that this outburst was a response to my failure to improve my technique after so many months and so many chances, and thus was of a kind with similar reactions I had induced over the years from piano teachers, dance instructors, football coaches, and the like, but this was just typical male egotism: the weeping was not about me at all. "It's my boyfriend," she gobbled, and then went on to tell me all about the cold and deceitful rat who never listened to her the way I did even though he could make her feel a way that no one else could, blah, blah, blah, etc., etc., etc.

When she paused for a particularly soggy nose-blowing session, I said,

"I'm glad you told me this," somehow knowing to leave off the rest: "...*now*. I'm glad you told me this *now*, rather than before, because I couldn't have managed even the puny little bit of genital intercourse that I just had with you. Really, that's quite enough information. Thank you."

Soon enough it was over, and Ingrid was having a beer down the hall with Arnie while I lay groaning and clawing my face in full Very Capable Kenny Jay post-pinning mode. Finally, I too returned to the party, if only to ensure that there was no danger of Arnie getting lucky. *Young Americans*, the default soundtrack for young Americans that spring, throbbed from the speakers.

"Why is it that we say *Fuck you* to an enemy or somebody we're pissed at?" Arnie asked.

"What do you mean?"

"It's like we're wishing them a pleasurable experience. I mean, wouldn't you say that to a friend instead? Like, when he's about to go out with some real lusty? *Oh, you're seeing Roxanne tonight? Well, hey! Fuck you!*"

"So what *should* we say to somebody we're pissed at?"

"I dunno... How about '*Unfuck you!*'?"

"What's *that* supposed to mean?"

"Like, 'I hope you *don't* get laid,' or maybe even, 'I'm taking away some lay you had in the past.'"

I was mortified. Could that actually work? Could a handful of *unfuck you*s pull me all the way back into the murky pit of virginity again, after all the agony I'd endured to claw my way clear of it?

"It's a powerful phrase," I remarked with a shudder. "Big medicine."

"Yeah, well, that's why they call it cursing. I mean, who cares if somebody yells *Fuck you!* at you anymore. You shrug it off, right? We need something fresh. Something with *bite*."

That night put a neat little period to my college education, and the next day I moved into the attic of a decrepit house on Spring Street to begin my new life as a full-fledged, fully employed member of Mankato society. I would never encounter Ingrid or her vagina again.[*]

---

[*] I got an email from her out of the blue just the other day, though. No last name, but it must have been her. She seemed very keen on letting me know about a new pharmaceutical product that would transform me into an unstoppable sexual monster for thirty-six hours. Better late than never, she probably figured.

9. Gerald Ford, Decade Slayer

Back in April, folk-rock hippie Shawn Phillips came to town for a concert at the student union. I glommed onto Haley and Margaux, who brought cheap red wine in a giant thermos. A warm-up joint inspired those two to explore bold new frontiers in face sucking, so I went walkabout, tiptoeing through the vast patchwork of territorial blankets and tablecloths that coated the floor of the high-vaulted hall while Shawn's roadies worked the stage.

One is never so plugged into one's college milieu as one is near the end of one's sophomore year. Every patch in this huge, motley quilt yielded a familiar face: a refugee from the quarter abroad here, a term paper client there, a napkin printing associate over yonder. More often than not the offer of a free toke, always accepted for the sake of decorum, followed a greeting.

Hedley G. Stonebridge then flickered into focus. He was my brother columnist at the *Reporter*, or so he reminded me on those rare occasions that our paths crossed. I thought of him more as my scary uncle columnist. He was old—ancient by student-newspaper-columnist standards: probably twenty-three. To me he personified the Sixties, or at least that portion of the Seventies that the Sixties had annexed. I assumed that assassinations, riots, and Ten Years After had been the wallpaper of his early college years, and that rock-heaving demonstrations, the death of former classmates in Vietnam and carefree sexual experimentation (the rumor that Hedley G. liked to be spanked had trickled down to those of us who did not covet such information) were all part of a day's work for him.

A generation gap—a chasm, really—had opened up between his age cohort and mine (My generation's whiny motto: "How come none of *my* friends ever gets drafted or killed? Is anything cinematic ever going to happen to *us?*"), but, astute as Hedley G. was about most matters, he appeared oblivious to this generational divide.

Hedley G. alarmed me because he set such very high standards. It was he who had interviewed Haley and others for the acclaimed exposé on a landlord who knowingly leased dangerously substandard housing to students; even more impressive, he had reportedly induced a plural number of women to actually spank him, despite a stark resemblance to an oven-braised sea lion.[*]

He certainly bore the burden of local fame better than I ever could. "What great ones do, the less will prattle of," one could imagine him shrugging, if one had the nerve to ask for confirmation on the spanking business. In contrast, I was having a devil of a time adjusting to my new *that-guy* status around town.

I was getting a lot of the *that-guy* treatment by April and not handling it well. When my name was called on the role in classes at the start of Spring Quarter, I found I had achieved the same eye-magnet quality that star athletes commanded, although the eyes that found me did not display envy or longing. They were the eyes of aquarium visitors perusing some hideous, newly discovered species of jellyfish.

Hedley G.—now there was a born that-guy. He thrived on local fame. Moreover, he cared passionately about stuff, and I didn't. I *wished* I did. I figured that someday I probably would. But as to what sort of stuff I might one day care passionately about, or when this elusive passion might kick in, I had no idea. I was just hoping that it would have the decency not to descend upon me in the midst of intercourse, though the odds of its striking during so infrequent and brief an event were long. More likely it would occur while I was clipping toenails.

In Hedley G.'s eyes, I had already arrived. After all, I was churning out

---

[*] In all fairness, this might have been a function of the weed and cheap wine.

Summer of Marv

six-hundred-word pieces devoid of spelling and syntax errors week after week. This alone, he assumed (and not without reason), vaulted me into the top percentiles of Mankato State denizens literacy-wise, and a literate person *must be* a political person.

Still, our column writing styles highlighted the yawning gap between us. A typical Hedley G. column would call out any public figure from the President down to an MSC dean for a systematic skewering with sharply honed facts dipped in Sixties vitriol. My idea of research for a column consisted of calling up random local celebrities like KEYC anchorman Chuck Pasek and asking them, "What do you think happens to us after we die?"*

This disparity in our styles did not seem to faze Hedley G. Surely, he thought, it was only a matter of time before this bright young man began to joust with the weightier subjects of corrupt Republicans, treacherous Democrats, racism, corporate greed, and above all, Nam.

"You can call the President of the United States a cruel and heartless son of a bitch and nobody gives a shit," snarled Hedley G., competing with a sound check on stage, "but if you dare attack their precious John Denver, oh *man*, just *watch* the mail pour in!" Spittle was now dangling in frothy streaks from the lush lower layer of his orange triple-canopy Fu Manchu. I had never before seen the cliché "working oneself into a lather" brought to life, but this bordered on the very thing.

What he had actually snarled was *Yukk'n CAW the PRIZZd'nt uh-thuh Ya-NYE-dud STAYZ a CRULL-un HAR-luss...* etc., for, like any concert-goer of his generation Hedley G. had partaken of at least one illegal substance by that stage of the evening and, like any future lifer of the Fourth Estate, he was already quite drunk as well.

I deciphered his grievance mainly from contextual clues. Earlier that

---

* As any Mankatoans who remember Chuck might expect, he handled this crude intrusion with the utmost aplomb: "Holy smoke! That—that's more than a question; that's a *philosophy!*" He was quick to admit that he had no idea what happens to us after we die. If Chuck has since found out, he has yet to share that scoop with the Key City viewing public, but God bless him just the same.

The Chuck-quoting column, titled "Fun With Death," still holds up reasonably well, I think, placing it in stark contrast with the bulk of my college oeuvre, which sucked with all the righteous, suckalicious suckiness that only college newspaper writing can, and generally does, suck with.

month, shortly after President Ford had requested that Congress provide emergency funding to the foundering South Vietnamese government in the hope of keeping it afloat a little longer, Hedley G. had indeed published a pluperfectly Stonebridgian piece which concluded that President Ford was, demonstrably, a cruel and heartless son of a bitch. In years past, this type of deliberately incendiary prose would have lit up both friends and foes like a fresh batch of napalm on the Ho Chi Minh trail. Letters of condemnation and support from similarly impassioned, ardently political readers would have flooded in. Now, there was only a deep, thrumming silence.

A few weeks later, Hedley G. decided to expend one of the few remaining columns of his collegiate career on a trifling topic, specifically a bemused assessment of the inexplicably popular John Denver tune "Thank God I'm a Country Boy." It was quite funny. Had we swapped genres, Hedley G. could have achieved much more success from slice-of-life material than I ever could have garnered in his domain.

I did not save his John Denver piece, but I recall a concise deconstruction of the chipper singer's background, proving that he was not, by any reasonable measure, a true country boy. There was the always fun, if inherently unfair, quoting of banal lyrics out of context. And there was a delightfully dismissive parting paragraph—declared "really good" by no less an authority than Nielsen: a single line suspended in space:

No, no, this simply will not do.

And *that* was the column that set off a record volume of hate mail, and *that* was why Hedley G. was bleary-eyed and soggy-mustached and at the edge of suicidal despair even before Shawn Phillips began to sing, and *that* was the moment that I realized that the Sixties had finally bought the big one—and not a moment too soon.

Long live the Seventies!

—¤—

It was all Ford's doing. Gerald R. Ford, that is: he was our president in 1975 through no fault of his own.

Ford was unique among presidents, as the Hedley G's of the world liked to point out, in that not a single citizen had voted him into national office. Wag that I was, I was wont to counter that he was also unique in that not a single citizen had voted against him for national office, either.

In like fashion, Ford would eventually become the president appreciated for all that he was *not* and for all that he did *not* do. Once pinned down in the Oval Office, he vigorously set about failing to whip inflation, eschewing sex with interns, flailing around Kenny Jay-like while Southeast Asia descended into chaos, not rescuing the crew of the SS Mayagüez from pirates, and, most famously, not getting shot.

The latter would prove to be his hallmark, his idiom, his forte. No president, not even the copiously fired-upon, eminently shootable Andrew Jackson, had previously managed to go oh-for-two in assassination attempts, and yet Gerald Ford would soon manage to set that standard during an astonishing cold streak in a single month.

But that would come later. In the spring of 1975 President Ford had become the focal point of much vituperation and loathing on college campuses—MSC included—because he was, after all, the President, and being loathed by smarty-pants college kids, then as now, was part of the job description.

Despite my best efforts, however, I failed at loathing Gerald Ford. No shame in that—most people failed at loathing him. But I tiptoed further into heresy by secretly starting to admire him.

Then again, *admire* is not the word. Better to say I empathized with him. For never in living memory had the congenital failures, clods and bunglers of our star-crossed democracy had representation in the highest office in the land until Gerald Ford lurched into it.

When the Chinese softened him up for negotiations by making him drink an individual toast with every single member of the Politburo, I thought *that's like me on a date with Jan Kelso*. Every time he banged his head on a helicopter doorway or barked his shin on its stairs, I, his natural constituent, felt a little less awkward about my sphincteral misfires inside Ingrid's vagina. And when, instead of waiting bolt upright for the kill shot in a gallant, Kennedyesque pose he ducked and shied and hobbled awkwardly away from would-be assassins, he was somehow redeeming me for driving down those damn railroad tracks. Gerald Ford shied for my shins.

At the end of the day, though, the most salient of Gerald Ford's non-attributes was his unloathability; for, for as long as my generation could remember, our President had been one of two lasciviously loathed personages. Johnson/Nixon simply could not be trusted, one was constantly being reminded by the Smarter People like Hedley G., and we had to constantly remain aware of what they were up to. That Johnson had been dead for two years and Nixon banished in disgrace was no excuse to let one's guard down.

By 1975, America was all loathed out. It needed a frivolous, throw-away president, a president who could just be part of the living room décor, and Gerald Ford obligingly assumed the role of Lampshade President. You sort of forgot he was there until he needed dusting or went slightly askew, throwing harsh light on you, and then you merely adjusted him and went back to poring over your Jaclyn Suzanne potboiler and otherwise got on with the business of your mundane existence.

And ironically enough, it was this very household-fixture quality that netted him the one positive achievement of his tenure: for it was Gerald Ford who finally killed the Sixties.

The Sixties—a great decade, a mind-blowing decade, a decade the likes of which could not have been imagined until it...it *unfolded* like some great *cosmic flower,* so *beautiful* and *pure*, when, like, *anything* could *just fuckin' happen, man!* and often *did!* Problem was that the Sixties weren't funny.* Moreover, the Sixties couldn't take a hint. You could cough and stretch and noisily clear the coffee table and mention having a big meeting early in the morning all you wanted: the Sixties weren't about to get up off your couch. Like an Allman Brothers drum solo, they just went on and on and on, eating up nearly half of the

---

* There is a moment on the Woodstock festival album when one of the performers sardonically dedicates a song to "the governor of California, Ronald RAY-GUNS!" That remark pretty neatly nutshelled Sixties irony.

Seventies, dragging their tedious Asian war and moribund presidents along with them, until Ford and his unloathability squashed the whole business and made political apathy at long last cool.

Lord knows he hadn't meant to do it. His house got whisked up in a tornado, and when he awoke—those rusty tufts of hair sticking out Bozo-like from the sides of his broad Midwestern mug—well, there were Johnson and Nixon and Rowan and Martin and Paul Revere and the Raiders all squashed flat underneath the gosh-darned thing.

And surveying the wreckage, we caretakers of this glittery, postmodern era, the Seventies, managed to pluck three jewels, the only contributions to civilization of the Sixties worth preserving: accessible drugs, Stevie Wonder, and of course bralessness.

10. Another Night on Front Street

Donna James did her bit to promote bralessness—and everything elselessness as well. But in this, she was merely fulfilling her contractual obligations as reigning default dancer at Mettler's down on Front Street.

Mettler's, God bless its soul, always offered a wholesome spiritual oasis from the other bars, a place where a weary youth could switch off a brain overtaxed by the dizzying triple whammy of alcohol, drugs, and female conversation. Life was ingeniously simplified in Mettler's: a single naked lady to contemplate as opposed to a roomful of the much more problematic clothed type. Donna James made no demands on you. She needed no mere man to make her dancing experience complete: she was fine on her own, thank you very much. And on any given night, a capacity crowd of ardent feminists was on hand to encourage her down this path of rugged individualism.

"Beaver!" one of them would call out, to which Nielsen's prompt response was: *"Badger!"*

On a typical night out on Front Street in the late spring of 1975, still well before the inevitable malling of the downtown district, your bar crawl would begin four blocks down from Mettler's at that generic college bar, the Hurdy Gurdy. Here you found the finest Happy Hour deals in town with *FREE POPCORN!*; yet ultimately, in a moment of clarity between seven and eight—Sad Hour—you would awake as if from a dream and see the place brimming with generic frat boys and sorority chicks. Later, a generic band

Summer of Marv

took to the generic stage and played generic covers, but you, a cultivated individual, would have been long gone by this time.

Across the street nothing was generic at the *sui generis* South Street Saloon, where factory workers and college kids together trod floorboards that had been soaking up spilled tap beer since the heyday of Hammurabi's acne. The South Street was always good for two rounds.

The Square Deal, which also shared the block, offered small, square tables on a crumpling linoleum floor. It was the Ingrid's vagina of bars, terrifying in its unpredictability, though much brighter inside—bright enough, in fact, to play cards in, as some patrons often did. One night the place would be overrun with haggard hippies who hadn't yet perused the memo on the demise of the Sixties; the next, a transient biker gang would rule the roost.

Having somehow survived the obligatory cameo at the Deal, you then proceeded down the long, arid stretch of Front Street—the Oran-to-Casablanca leg of the refugee trail, utterly barless but for the deliciously seedy Club Royal—all of it turf which you and your associates had marked off for yourselves over the years, often in a most primal manner. Here was the jewelry store behind which Arnie and Haley's roommate Barry had been arrested on suspicion of breaking and entering, the charge later corrected to public urination; over there the ancient movie theater from which Nielsen and Durward had been evicted for laughing too boisterously during the vigilante execution scenes of *Magnum Force*. You could go on and on: Memm'ries, like the corners of your mind…

—◻—

Two doors past Mettler's, that was where it stood, the place to which all roads led: to this paragon of watering holes, this precious jewel, this *other* other Eden: this blessed dive, this earth, this realm, this Rathskeller! Or just "the Rat's" to its friends.[*]

Under a red neon martini glass, you shouldered open a sticky front door and entered a stoner Batcave. You let your eyes adjust, stared down a long

---

[*] And by this point in the evening's festivities, you were hardly of a mind to attempt to articulate the word *Rathskeller*, anyway.

row of stools, and immediately made out three or four familiar faces day or night at any given time, some of which were really there. In the ballroom, regional stalwarts City Mouse and Judd played on a high stage in the flicker of a rotating glitter-ball while dancers danced and real men stole their drinks.

You could go on and on but... Your power to describe the charm of the Rat's was to be forever hobbled by the perpetual dimness of both the place itself and that of your senses through all the hours of all the nights of all the years spent therein. What it was is best left to the individual's imagination. But whatever it was, neither time nor distance could ever erode a jot of its charm. It was, in short, what I fully expect Heaven to look, sound, and smell like, albeit without those annoying "Last call" cries.

—¤—

...All of which brings you—us—back to Mettler's, where, as already noted, one could watch a real live lady take off nearly all her clothes. Not a lot of ladies, mind you, just one, Donna James as often as not—over and over again, night after night, for a week, after which Donna vanished for a spell and another naked lady took charge but never quite seemed to belong. The crowd would glare balefully at this naked interloper with eyes that said *You're not our real mom* and Durward would spout mean poetry at her until she went away.

The air here was smokier and thicker than that of the Rat's, and so was the clientele. It was a long, narrow establishment: a college lad in training could do a triple-jump across it. In the corner just inside the back door stood an illuminated stage, toward which all the swollen stomachs in the place swerved like so many sunflowers on a dewy June morning when our *belle du jour* (actually *belle du week*) emerged from her subterranean nest to grace us with the privilege of watching her same old bosoms spill from yet another plumed and bespangled costume like two molten pyroclastic flows threatening to engulf the slack-jawed villagers below.

All tables close to said stage would have long since been staked out by bloated local men in work-clothes or leisure suits by the time we shuffled in. Earlier in the evening these men had clicked the opening rounds of bottled Schlitzes together and griped about the petty indignities of their jobs. Now they slumped limply in those chairs, legs dangling lifelessly in front of them. Their bloated, slack-jawed heads, bathed in the flashing red and orange stage lights, lolled on thick latex stalks as if watching the departure of the spaceship which had just returned them to earth after a draining cavity probe.

"*Beaver!*" a self-nominated spokesman for the tribe would bark—it could have been any one of them at any time, thus bearing out chaos theory—to which Nielsen would bellow back "*Otter!*" with equal assurance.

On this night Nielsen, Arnie and I occupied a booth near the front door, remote from the stage, and ordered roast beef sandwiches. Currently writhing to the Wings hit "Silly Love Songs," Donna James modeled a sheer pink see-through negligee and a crimson-spangle-encrusted G-string. We arrived just in time for a key plot point, the loosening of the negligee. The G-string, according to some damn fool regulations, would have to remain in place, but if the lads nearest the stage would remain appreciative and civil, Donna might find a loophole.

At the end of the tune, the negligee was, as forecast, unfastened to riotous hooting and Pavlovian orders of more bottles of Schlitz and Miller High Life. Mettler's patrons drank hard. They drank, like middle-aged men the world over, to forget: to forget their squandered youth, to forget their miserable dead-end jobs, to forget their mounting debts, and, most urgently, to forget what Donna James's breasts looked like so that they could get excited all over again the next time those parabolic sacs flopped forth. Some of these men had a more encyclopedic knowledge of Donna James's topography—her contours, her landmarks, her escarpments and peaks—than they had of their own wives', so the forgetting didn't come easy. They had to work at it, and that meant investing in an awful lot of Schlitz. Then again, we only go around once in life.

Donna stuck with Paul McCartney: next up was "Listen to What the Man Says," during which the negligee fell to the floor. It was a bouncy tune, so Donna bounced. She bounced well for a woman of her vintage, and this elicited polite yowling from the drooling throng.[*] But inevitably, like tourists

---

[*] It is impossible to define *polite yowling* beyond stating that it is a high-pitched exhortation coaxed from the throats of inebriated but harmless middle-aged Mankato males when confronted with the nearly nude and bouncing body of a fit, ovulating, raven-haired stripper.

staring too long at the ceiling of the Sistine Chapel, the crowd itched to move on and behold still greater wonders.

"*Beaver!*" someone hollered.

"*Muskrat!*" retorted Nielsen.

"*Bea-VER!*" insisted another regular, looking askance at us.

"*Hamster!*" I countered.

"*Mollusk!*" Arnie chimed in.

Nielsen groaned. "The fuck you yellin' *mollusk* for?"

"*Wha*-at? Can't I yell *mollusk?*"

"No, Arnie, you can't." I interjected. "It has to be a mammal."

"Who says? I thought it just had to be somethin' furry," said Nielsen, further muddying the waters.

"Right," I said. "A small, furry mammal. Although it's sort of redundant if you think about it, since a mammal is by definition furry."

"Hold on," said Arnie, trying to get his own back. "I don't think that's always true."

There ensued a lengthy discussion, the type of which can only occur in the premier gentlemen's club of a college town, in which I defied the others to try to name either an unfurry mammal or a fur-bearing non-mammal. Vaguely fuzzy-looking fungi and microorganisms were swiftly ruled out.

The discussion was momentarily suspended by the arrival of our sandwiches, steaming mounds of freshly dynamited cow scooped straight off the pasture onto soggy buns. Whether or not it was advisable to allow these entrees to seep into our molecular essences ought to have been the subject of an entirely new debate, but at this stage in the evening, having recently sampled Arnie's powerful Cities-export marijuana in the Rat's parking lot, we simply dove in.

"The point is," I concluded between chews, "*mollusk* is out of the question."

"Yeah," said Nielsen, his lips so spackled with cow shrapnel that they could have been roped off as a bovine crime scene, "I concur. Never seen no hair on a fuckin' mollusk."

"But the deeper point is, why *beaver?* Does that"—here I gestured in the general direction of Donna James's venerated reproductive organs—

"resemble a beaver any more than it does, say, a possum or a muskrat?"

"Okay, I see what you mean," said Arnie.

"Beaver!" insisted a tomato-headed patron with growing resolve. The cry was picked up by his fellows:

"BEEEE-VER! BEEEE-VER! BEEEE-VER!..."

And then from Donna's nether regions sprang blinding lasers. It was the lights catching her spangled G-string as she ever so briefly pulled it down to offer the addled masses a glimpse of the Promised Land.

There was a long instant of stunned silence followed by a uniform hoot of approval, spiked with hoarse cries of *"Beaver! Beaver!"*, for these are men who know it when they see it. And then it was gone. In a blinding, spangly flash, the highlight of their week had passed.

"You guys, what do you think?" Arnie said. "Suppose that from the earliest times girls and women, like, went around with their whole torsos exposed, but always kept their kneecaps covered up," he said. "Do you think there'd be, like, this whole industry built up around women showing their kneecaps?"

"Kneecaps!" bellowed Nielsen, trying it on for size. *"KneeCAPS!"*

"Well, in that case men wouldn't yell *'Kneecaps!'"* I said.

"How come?"

"Think about it. The way it is now, do they yell *Pubic region!* or *Vagina!?*"

"No," said Nielsen, ruminating over shreds of ruminant, "but maybe we oughtta start!"

"I think they'd throw us out," I said. "They barely tolerate *Groundhog!*"

"So what *would* they yell instead of *Kneecaps!?*"

"Some kind of metaphor," said Arnie.

"I think you mean a synecdoche."

"Huh?"

"What the fuck kind of animal looks like a kneecap, anyway?"

This question led us into a long, chewy interlude as Donna scooped up her scattered wardrobe and made a stately egress toward her basement HQ. Finally:

"Wanna go back to the Rat's?"

"Yeah."

Josh Muggins

The kneecap question would have to wait until fall, when all roads would lead back to Katoland and we could reconvene this jury for another night on Front Street.

11. Meanwhile, Back on Spring Street

"You know who you look like?" Rosa asks me, batting away a mosquito.

"I have a feeling you're going to tell me."

Little sister Laura giggles precognitively as Rosa clobbers me with:

"*Greg Gagne!*"

"What?? *Noooooooooo!*" I cry, tipping backward in my vinyl lawn chair from the force of the blow.

"You *do!* You *do!* You look just like *Greg Gagne!*"

I marvel now, from the perspective of middle age, that I should have taken such umbrage at the comparison. Greg Gagne was, after all, a young professional athlete, fit and trim, as his weekly bouts seen on the local ABC affiliate demonstrated. He was also the son and heir apparent of American Wrestling Association shogun Vern Gagne and partner of Jim Brunzell in the tag team known for their daring acrobatic leaps and soaring drop-kicks as the High Flyers: an all-American boy in eentsy black tights.

From the Mexican-teenage-girls-next-door POV, the comparison was surely intended as a compliment; but for us smarty-pants college types, the High Flyers were earnest wienies whose colorless interviews soaked up precious broadcast minutes that might have been expended on Nick Bockwinkle or Baron von Raschke. Oh, compare me not to

Greg Gagne, girls. Let it be Bockwinkle or the Baron,[*] or Mad Dog Vachon, or Superstar Billy Graham, or even that queeny old gasbag Larry "the Ax" Hennig.

Would that someone would compare me to any of them now.

Lo these many years have I searched for other females with whom I could while away the hours of a torpid, mosquito-plagued summer evening comparing notes on AWA warriors—even unto, on occasion, reenacting a Greco-Roman Knuckle Lock or Sleeper Hold (but never a Pile Driver or an Airplane Spin, because those moves were *banned in some states and should be in this one*—and Rosa and Laura, after all, were ladies), and yet in vain. Vanity of vanities; all is vanity.

—¤—

The ad in the *Reporter* sought a "mellow male or female to share large house." I reckoned I was one of those.

What I found was a compact foursquare structure on a street within walking distance—or staggering distance, as Mr. Arboleda was apt to demonstrate—of downtown. In the Twenties perhaps this old neighborhood had been central to the growing burg, but the Key City bourgeoisie had long since fled the flood plain for the outlying hills.

An enclosed porch clogged with inert appliances led to a cavernous parlor and dining room. A huge bespattered gray-and-white striped sofa lay in a mote-laden sunbeam by the front window. A rocking chair identical to the one that the inscrutable Mrs. Arboleda occupied on the open porch next door and the brain-dead remains of a Westinghouse TV rounded out the ground-floor furnishings. In a lamentable lapse of judgment, I would place my eight-track stereo system here for communal use to fill the entertainment void.

The dark hardwood flooring and intricate woodworking throughout the

---

[*] Durward chose to live out a good portion of his college life in the persona of Jim "the Baron" Raschke out of Omaha—*Zee Baron vill now apply zee Klaaaww!*—essentially a big, wild Midwestern boy doing a big, wild, Midwestern man doing a Nazi war criminal hiding out in the AWA.

ground floor had admirably withstood decades of inattention, as had the architect's pride and joy, a flared and elegantly railed staircase. A faint aroma that may have been ancient river water fought its way through a fruity veneer of incense.

"You can move into one of the bedrooms when somebody moves out," came Al's voice, drifting to me across a galaxy of dust motes in the attic, "but this is all we got for now. The forty-five bucks covers utilities. Nan'll collect your share. Just make sure you never give it to Marnie. No matter what she says, nothing to Marnie: remember that."

"Got it."

"If Nan's up, I'll introduce you. I don't know where the other girls are. They're usually around in the daytime."

"Are they students?"

Al looked at me as though I had suggested my new housemates might be Mennonites or astral projectors or yak herders.

"No. They all work on and off at massage parlors and saunas and such in the area." He paused in his descent of the ladder that accessed the attic to make mirthless eye contact. "Hope that's not a problem."

No, I assured him, I could be counted on to harbor no bias against women of that trade.

"I keep a room here but I spend most of my time at my woman's house," Al informed me en route to present me to the three accomplished manual technicians with whom I'd be sharing the house.

The excitement was palpable. I was already playing out *Dating Game* scenarios in my head in which I got to ask questions like "Housemate Number Two, complete this sentence: 'I love giving my male housemate gratis handjobs more than *blank*.'"

Such reveries quickly melted away as I shook hands with the statuesque Nan, however. I could feel her Fu Manchu staring daggers downward into my sparser one, and I had a policy about women who could do that. Still, two more to go. The odds remained in my favor. One of them had to be the type to throw a starving man a manual-gratification freebie now and then.

Alas, Marnie was exactly that type. Though probably in her mid-twenties,

Marnie's arms had acquired fourth-grade-teacher jiggle-bags, the untamed undulations of which might provoke seasickness in the throes of a spirited handjob—a hypothesis I was not inclined to test.

The last housemate, Cheryl, was…nice. She had nice blond hair. One simply scrambled for nice things to say about Cheryl because she was so gosh-darned *nice*. Nonetheless, any journalistically fair and balanced description of Cheryl would be incomplete without noting that her dimensions were those of a packing crate capable of shipping Marnie, Nan, and me with room to spare for a small card table.

—¤—

"Ya get yer mattress back up there okay?" came Marnie's voice one languid June night, once again addressing me from the inky void of her bedroom as I made my way back from the bathroom.

"Yeah. I found it in Al's room."

"It was the fire marshal again."

"You told me."

"It's a pain in the ass draggin' it down through that little trapdoor every time."

And no can of corn shoving it back up, I wanted to say. The ladder to my attic lair stood just outside Marnie's bedroom door; I groped madly in the dark for it now.

The fire marshal was a frequent guest in the daytime, while I was at work, and it fell upon the underemployed Marnie to convince him that no one was residing illegally in the attic. Ergo, she was now fishing for gratitude for her Herculean efforts to spare me from eviction. But my priority at the moment was to elude her clutches.

"Hot up there, huh?" she said.

"Yeah," I replied, finally snagging a rung.

"I got this big ol' fan on. Nice 'n breezy in here," she continued, in a melodic version of her guttural chain-smoker's rasp, and at that moment I grasped that within seconds, crucial seconds, she would reach for a cigarette and strike a match, which would illuminate her stark naked body, sprawled on the sheetless mattress like a gassy, viscous continent riding uneasily atop a thick tectonic plate. "You oughtta come in and—"

But by then I was shutting my trapdoor and wondering, not for the first time, if I were a sufficiently mellow male or female to share this house after all.

—¤—

Cary and Hoppy and I, now working full eight-hour days at Pearlman's, established a custom of lunching at Harry's Hofbrau Haus, hidden away in the recesses of the decrepit Burton Hotel beyond a curious tableau of petrified retirees who had taken root on sofas in the lobby. We would blow past their vampiric Coke-bottle stares and pillage Harry's turkey-and-roast-beef-anchored all-you-can-eat noon buffet. It would sometimes constitute my only real meal of the day, since any groceries I tried to store at home vanished as if into a black hole. Sauna work evidently burned a lot of carbs. Who knew?

Late afternoons, Rosa and Laura would bound forth like foxhound pups when they saw the Missile pull up on Spring Street. Jack and Larry, long-haired freelancers who were repainting the Arboledas' house that summer at a pace that would have made Pope Julius II think more fondly of Michelangelo, used this combusting excitement as an excuse to knock off work on those occasions when they might be caught still at it, and a long, slow Frisbee toss invariably broke out among the five of us, plus sundry other Arboledas who might emerge. The family was Mexican but their house a Russian novel, constantly disgorging characters whom you were never quite sure whether or not you had encountered before.

We would station ourselves on either side of the street and curve our tosses around the mature elms that lushly shaded the block, or skim them off the cars parked along the street—even off passing vehicles as the weeks passed and our boldness grew.

Later Jack and Larry would pull their cooler over to the lawn chairs that, along with two stumps, formed a circle on the Arboledas' treeless and grassless front yard. Mrs. Arboleda would mend clothes and watch the girls,

Madame Defarge-like, as they watched the shirtless, tattooed painters drink beer and smoke cigarettes.

At twilight Mr. Arboleda would stagger into view at the end of the block, ever unwilling to abandon his awful impersonation of sobriety, and pass silently into his house. He broke character only once, when the sight of his painters, seated on his tree stumps with dozens of discarded cigarette ends at their feet and blatantly not painting, seemed to make him snap.

"Get your *butts* off my lawn," he rasped.

Jack and Larry began to rise, silently accepting their overdue return to the ranks of the unemployed.

Mr. Arboleda shook his head, gestured stiffly at the scattered cigarette ends, and repeated: "Get your *butts*...off my lawn!"

Then he bent double with lung-rattling guffaws and sauntered jauntily into his house to continue the plodding assassination of his own brain. He had just made his first joke in English. No one had the heart to point out to him that the term "lawn" connoted an expanse of land supporting at least some traces of living vegetation. Let him have his moment.

—¤—

Our improvised games of Frisbee, touch football, and wrestling resumed just after the Arboleda family's dinner and continued until it was too dark to see. Then we retired to the circle of chairs under the great ailing elm that towered over our adjoining properties for a cooling session of repartee perhaps not unlike those enjoyed a generation earlier by the literati of the Algonquin Round Table, except with sagging vinyl lawn chairs and Mexican teens.

As the day drew to a close, the absence of my mattress would sometimes tell me that my arch-foe the fire marshal had dropped by once again.

Why this personal vendetta, I wondered. I'd never even met the man. He always made his inspections while I was at work, so I was destined never to confront him. I tried to picture him, but the only marshals that I knew of were Marshal Dillon of *Gunsmoke* fame and the marshal of the Stratego board game, a sour-looking chap with a squinty profile and black whiskbroom moustache and feathery lampshade on his head. Only a Spy or a Bomb could

Summer of Marv

kill him. I shuddered at the thought of acquiring so ferocious an adversary.

Once I had finally stuffed the mattress back up through the trapdoor again, I scooted it to the side of the attic that faced the street. The window afforded a view of the yard through the interstices of gnarly elm branches that rustled pleasantly against the porch roof in the night breezes. The propensity for post-coital smoking on the floor beneath me on those surprisingly frequent nights when Marnie, possessor of unsuspected Circe-like powers and that very large fan, induced a stoned house painter or two to stay with her, led me to visualize the elm branches as a potential escape route should the fire marshal's worst fears (or greatest hopes) come true.

Visualization of another sort inevitably came over me on those sticky summer nights. Lynn, a petite sophomore from Meldom, lived just around the corner on Broad. I ran into her from time to time, always assuring myself that I would take advantage of our proximity the next chance I got. In the meantime, she was in heavy rotation on Fantasy Hit Parade all through June along with assorted dental hygienists. Jan Kelso had by then been relegated to Oldies Night.

What I didn't see coming was the meteoric rise to number one of Rosa Arboleda—she of the curtain of astonishingly glossy black hair and the tiny heart-shaped face. At sixteen she just didn't seem ready for the responsibility that the top slot entailed, her willingness and ability to execute a Double Vertical Forward Suplex on me notwithstanding.

Eventually I persuaded myself that it was permissible to lust for Rosa, if only in the privacy of my thoughts, as long as I kept Laura the hell out of there. Laura claimed to be fourteen, but I suspected that this meant something along the lines of "fourteen next February." She was already taller and lankier than Rosa in a strikingly non-Arboleda way (Mr. and Mrs. A were constructed close to the ground), and incredible beauty was obviously knocking on the door; within a year or two it would surely smash its way through, and she would become irresistible. But for now, and for the foreseeable future, she remained on the blacklist.

So that was settled: I now gave my thoughts free rein re Rosa. I set my pillow on the window ledge and dangled my right arm into the sultry night breeze while my left went about its usual nocturnal business, and the ancient elms swayed drunkenly, and the radio poured 10cc into my ear:

I'm not in love,
So don't forget it.
It's just a silly phase I'm going through.
And just because I call you up,
Don't get me wrong,
Don't think you've got it made.
I'm not in love, no no...

Yet another whimper of mellow yearning in a year that had already seen the Eagles give us the best of their love, Joe Cocker assure us that we were so beautiful to him, and Frankie Valli confide that his eyes adored us—perhaps inspiring Neil Sedaka to hear laughter in the rain. And after all that, Olivia Newton-John had the effrontery to ask if we had never been mellow. One hankered to unleash a full platoon of Funky Chinamen from Funky Chinatown upon that cheeky Aussie concubine.

Still, I liked the soothing lilt of the 10cc song, a tune that for me would forever define the summer of the Arboleda girls. Its beat set a nice pace for the deed at hand, too. And just as things seemed to be moving along about as well as could be expected, there came a scratchy cry from below:

"Hey, Josh! Whatcha doin'?"

There are awkward moments in life, and then there are the truly mortifying moments. And lurking even beyond those moments, there comes that true crucible: the chilling instant when the teenage neighbor to whose image you are pleasuring yourself appears in real life before your eyes and asks:

Hey, whacha doin'?

10cc wasn't helping the situation at all:

I keep your picture upon the wall.
It hides a nasty stain that's lying there.

Alas, I had no picture of Rosa upon my wall—to this day it remains a source of no small quantity of remorse that I retain no totems at all of the Arboleda clan, and in some ways it makes their very existence seem as mythical as the Aztec deities to whom their collateral virgin ancestors, less adept at AWA-approved self-defense tactics than the surviving gene pool, were sacrificed atop pyramids—but here, at this moment, a very real Rosa stood before me, all silky-haired and olive-skinned and virginal, calling up to me from the yard below as if we were a transposed and less iambic Romeo and Juliet. It was one of the most pressure-packed situations I'd found myself in throughout an already long, illustrious masturbatory career. And yet I managed to reply "Oh, just hanging out" and somehow pulled it off.

Ha-ha! "Pulled it off!"

Mr. Arboleda, that enthusiast of English word-play, surely would have winked his approval.

12. Big Red Machine

The outlook wasn't brilliant for the Pearlman's napkin-printing nine on Opening Night. That was clear the moment we looked across the Wheeler Park diamond and saw that cattle-call tryouts for a Shakespeare in the Park production of *Henry IV* were in progress along the opposite foul line.

These were the great gouty men of a local sheet metal shop, most of them well into the second decade of their Industrial League careers and the third beers of the evening even before the first slow pitch had been lobbed.

We would counter these assorted Pistols and Petos with our tired, our poor, and our retching Lenny Kortig as starting pitcher because most of our likeliest men had declined to sign on. "*Slow*-pitch? *Hah!*" snorted Chad, the lycanthropic line manager, when I inquired into his absence from our first and only practice. Even some of our frat boys considered the Industrial League beneath their dignity. So we few; we scrawny few; we band of napkin-printing brothers remained to hoist the Pearlman's banner and face down the barbarian horde. I saw us as greyhounds on the base paths, if we could only *get* on base.

We would soon learn that slow-pitch softball is a sport that favors the gouty over the greyhound. In the first inning a massive sheet-metalista clubbed a shot so far over our centerfielder's head that the ball did not meander back to the infield until long after the perpetrator had completed a leisurely tour of the bases and ostentatiously cracked open a celebratory Schlitz.

Our opponents were great home run trotters, employing the trot even when trying to beat out infield hits. When our infield proved competent enough to throw such trotters out, they cavalierly trotted off the field to be rewarded with yet more infusions of Schlitz. Schlitz's advertising campaign famously observed that we only go around once in life and are thus obliged to reach out and grab for all the gusto we can. Our opponents clearly were incorrigible gusto-grabbers. They managed to be at once the looser team and the tighter one.

I rode the bench for Manager-for-Life Marv through four long, brutal innings—or would have, had there been a bench. Denied the dignity of actual bench-riding, we reserves milled about in our cutoff jeans and muttered darkly as yet another of Lenny's offerings found the heart of an opponent's bat with a dull metallic *thunk!* and soared prettily through the June twilight, while our outfielders stood as transfixed as if watching a meteor shower. Lenny's lone qualification as pitcher was his ability to read and give signs, a skill he had honed on nights when excessive alcohol shut down his brain's speech center, forcing him to resort to an elaborate idiolect of gestures to communicate his needs. Alas, there are no signs in slow-pitch softball, all pitches being slowballs, so this skill profited us naught.

Down ten to one by the top of the fifth, Marv pulled several of his cronies to keep him company and put in Cary, Hoppy and me as sacrifices to the slow-pitch gods. I suddenly found myself leading off the inning.

This was the moment that I had visualized every night in my attic lair for the preceding week, temporarily fending off intrusive thoughts of Mexican teens, Meldom girls, dental hygienists and Linda Ronstadt.

I stepped to the plate, trembling with anticipation. Or with something. Whatever I was trembling with, I felt sure the knocking of my knees was not that noticeable, while at the same time lamenting the fashion statement of jeans cut off at the thigh.

"*Ooooh*, look at them creamy liddle legs!" came a smarmy voice from first base. It was the flame-bearded man-mountain who had clubbed the first-inning home run. Initially lost in the crowd of Eastcheap tavern habitués, this Falstaffian figure suddenly seemed oddly familiar. "Them creamy white legs is *a-shakin'!* We *got* him!" continued Sir John, as assorted Bardolfs and Nyms chortled along. "Oh, *hell*, yeah! We *got* this purdy boy!" Suddenly I found myself locked into one of those hideous adolescent nightmares where one realizes one's nakedness all too late in the midst of a public function.

A pitch sailed high and was called a ball. Cary applauded my good eye. The next pitch fluttered down just like the one in my vision—the one I was meant to launch straight over the leaping shortstop's glove. I swung and fouled it back. The waterlogged catcher lunged for it but missed. Nobody commented on my eye this time, but my knees had turned to Schlitz foam, and the taunting crescendoed. The immense scarlet fur-ball at first base compared my swing unfavorably to the swishing of a passing squirrel's tail.

The third pitch was the right one. There was the jolt and the tell-tale *ping* of contact, and in an instant the ball was sailing over the inbred shortstop's… shadow. He knocked the ball down on the first bounce but lost it momentarily in the webbing of his throwing hand. I reached on an error. So much for batting a thousand, though my on-base percentage was pristine.

Hoppy gave me a nasal *Way to go!* while Cary noted that I had gotten something started and Marv, annoyed at this senseless dragging-out of our destruction, leaned on the hood of his car and regaled his henchmen with Polack jokes while glancing at his watch. Meanwhile, down at first base, my tormenter was similarly unmoved by my batsmanship. "Hey, kid," he chimed, "Give yuh a quarter tuh kiss my ass."

The outdoor context and the cap had thrown me off. Sure enough, it was my old Yum Yum nemesis, Red. Any doubt was quickly put to rest by his teammates. *"Don't scare the kid, Red!" "You'll hafta clean up after 'im if 'e pisses on yer base, Red!"*

When Motzie knocked a grounder several yards foul I sprinted around second before pulling up and skulking sullenly back to Red's domain, where the ass-kissing transaction was yet again brought to the table. For some reason I found Red's failure to remember me from Yum Yum days—as evidenced by his return to a mere quarter, the opening position which we had long since abandoned when negotiations stalled due to my resignation—even more off-putting than his indelicate comments on my legs. I wondered if he had found other college boys to harass since our separation, if he regarded me as nothing more than an old notch in a very large belt. In any event, I no longer felt special.

Motzie popped out. Cary drove the ball deep, but directly at a wobbly Bardolf out in left. I died at first in more ways than one.

At Marv's capricious decree, I stayed in the game at catcher, a position I had never played in my life. I did not crave the spotlight on defense. Let me cower in right field, my natural habitat, the Pluto of the softball solar system, where I could occasionally pound my glove, yell encouragement that might reach the pitcher's ears a light-year later, and otherwise drift harmlessly in my erratic orbit.

Cary, in relief of Lenny, induced a slow roller back to himself to dispatch the first batter. He brought to the mound the revolutionary conviction that his role was to get batters out, not merely to put the ball in play. It might have been easier to judge his effectiveness, however, had he not been pitching mainly to over-lubricated late-inning substitutes.

The next hitter, another sub, likewise made sweet contact on a back-spun pitch, resulting in a meek grounder to short. He cursed and hurled his bat on my feet, but to his own surprise ended up on first when our shortstop, also a late-inning sub, chose that moment to show off his dead-on tunnel impression.

That brought Red to the plate.

"*One down!*" I felt compelled to shout, and had great plans to expand on the remark with "*Come on, come on! Easy out! Easy out!*" when Red preempted me with a jaunty *sotto voce* "Shut the fuck up, kid."

Red, unruffled by Cary's backspin, launched a rocket over Bart Stoltz's parallelogram-shaped head in left. My personal reaction was one of relief in that Red now departed my bailiwick with all the haste that a gouty, beanbag-chair-shaped sheet metal worker could muster. But as the old saw goes, everything that goes around, comes around. So it is with men's misdeeds; so it is with their acts of kindness; and so it is with clamorous, porous-brained slow-pitch sluggers pining for the last Schlitz in the cooler.

The first man scored easily, eclipsing my view of the action as he waddled past. But behind this human moon a horrific tableau unfolded in the gathering gloom as Red and the ball raced—for lack of a better word—toward home plate, the former now rounding third and the latter sailing in from the park's outer precincts. I blocked the plate. Sheet metal workers guffawed in a rising *basso profundo* triad. Red licked his lips. At the last minute, Hoppy, the cut-off man—actually the last in a bucket brigade of cut-off men—spared my skeletal integrity by throwing wildly over the backstop, thus excusing me from plate-blocking duty at the last second.

By the time I had retrieved the ball, the Mercy Rule had been invoked to obviate the need for further innings of humiliation. Red cracked open that coveted last Schlitz as though it were the skull of a vanquished medieval foe, Marv yawned something that may have been "Let life be short, else shame will be too long," and soon my fellow reserves and I were bound for the first of many postgame drownings of sorrows at the Rat's.

13. Meanwhile, Back in Meldom

The humiliation of Opening Night was assuaged somewhat the following Saturday morning as I found myself piloting the Missile toward that lustrous pearl of the prairie, Meldom, Minnesota, with the sleek high-back bucket seat to my right occupied by the equally well-upholstered Lynn.

I had run into Lynn near her residence on Broad Street—a chance encounter after consecutive evenings of aerobic loitering there—and heard her wistfully bemoan her lack of means to get back to her hometown that weekend for her brother's birthday, to which comment I had remarked on what astounding coincidences life presents, as I was slated to be in Meldom myself to see Nielsen and Durward. This would be news to Nielsen and Durward, but the lads had always shown admirable flexibility toward such antiquated social niceties as formal invitations.

In the car Lynn prattled on about long unseen family members—her cousin, this; her grandmother, that—while I nodded and laughed at appropriate intervals and mentally undressed her from the top down, then from the bottom up, and finally from side to side, which was more challenging. Eventually I pictured us lying naked on my mattress as I gravely intoned, "And the *two* shall become *one!*" or some such wedding-napkin sentiment as prelude to sliding in safe at home.

These reveries were interrupted by the irksome jerking of the Missile whenever it automatically shifted gears to clear one of the rolling hillocks that rumple the landscape of southwestern Minnesota. "You oughtta get that looked into," advised Lynn. I nodded but was unconcerned. We had already passed the city limits sign, and over the next rise lay Meldom proper, the burg with the highest per capita concentration of motorheads in the free world. Just let the word slip out that a Dodge Challenger engine somewhere in town needed looking into, and the only problem one faced would be prodding all the would-be diagnosticians into an orderly line. Tom Sawyer-like, I could easily end up charging them for the privilege of poking around under my hood.

And as we crested the next hill Meldom did indeed come into view on the distant horizon, just as a clamorous pinging and thunking broke out under the Missile's hood as though a squad of drunken sheet-metal workers were taking batting practice inside.

I had just popped the hood and begun feigning comprehension of of the hissing, mist-enshrouded clutter that greeted my eyes when Kyle Olafson, yet another Meldomite from the dorm floor, cruised by in a shiny, black, eminently functional Chevy Cheyenne pickup. He U-turned, greeted us with a toss of his Leif Garrett hair and a wry peep over his reflector shades, made off with Lynn, and promised to send help.

I was just about parboiled in the front seat by the time an august personage named Herman, Meldom's reigning Motorhead Laureate, was chauffeured to the scene by Nielsen. Herman grimly surveyed the Missile's steaming innards for thirty seconds before handing down his assessment: "She's tossed her cookies." Nielsen seconded it. I said that that didn't sound good, and was rewarded with a flattering comparison of my deductive powers with those of Sherlock Holmes. Herman glanced at his watch and called it: Time of death, eleven-oh-nine a.m.

Nielsen tried to console me as best he could by ensuring that I remained thoroughly anesthetized and armed the whole weekend on his family ranch. But it was pointless. The whole town seemed in mourning. When a 340 six-pack tosses its cookies on their terrain, Meldomites react with the same spiritual solemnity as Fenimore Cooper's Mohicans at the slaying of a deer.

It fell upon Durward to drive me back to Mankato in his pickup Sunday afternoon. Along the way he summarized the dual plotlines of his own summer: working all day at the local lawn mower plant while, as a voluntary sideline, cultivating an immense ditchweed crop on an unused tract of the family ranch. At the plant he attached some sort of doohickey to mowers as they passed by him on an assembly line. He related with pride how he had barely managed to show up one morning following an especially patriotic night at the Meldom American Legion, later vomiting vigorously into an arbitrarily selected burlap bag without halting the line or missing a single unit.

As a storyteller Durward was gifted with the capacity to place the listener almost corporeally into the scene he was describing, which was usually diverting but in this instance unfortunate. It just made a tragic weekend feel even more so, especially when he insisted on reenacting the burlap bag sequence while speeding along a busy two-lane highway.

—◻—

Thus began a long, hot summer of angry dependency, as I had to rely on the kindness of napkin printers for transport to work, to softball games, and to anywhere else I wanted to go. I was pretty much stuck at home evenings, which wasn't all that bad thanks to the neighbor girls.

"All right, here's one for you," I said very late one night. "'You're so ugly...'"

"Okay, okay. 'You're so ugly, when you were born the doctor slapped your parents.'"

"Good! How about this one: 'You're so fat...'"

"That's easy. 'You're so fat that when you dance, the *band* skips.'"

"Good, good."

"Or, 'You're so fat that people jog around you for exercise.'"

"Yes, that'll do nicely."

"Or, 'You're so fat that when you sit—'"

"That'll *do*."

The ancient elm sighed as a cool night breeze stroked it, snapping me out of Rosa's spell. A full day of work and another softball debacle lay ahead. Amusing as it had been to drill Rosa with a paperback compendium of all-purpose insults, the better to arm her for verbal combat with her haughty, native-born adversaries once high school began again, my thoughts now inclined toward my mattress.

It was cool enough at this hour that the metal, seashell-backed lawn chair, which served a purely punitive function by day, could be safely occupied. I rocked forward in it.

Rosa, sensing my inclination to retire, sought to keep me pinned down by means less direct than the usual Half Nelson supplemented with armpit tickling.

"Come *on*," she pleaded, leaning in so that her knees grazed mine, "gimme a *hard* one."

"Okay, try this one: 'You're so *skinny* that…'"

"You're so skinny that…"—she cast her gaze skyward and poked her tongue out of the corner of her mouth—"that you could fall through your asshole and hang yourself."

"Good! Very good! Not in the book, but…that's neither here nor there."

I gave her a smile of approbation, which she reflected back at me.

"Josh," she said, "you got a girlfriend?"

I sputtered for a while until coming to grips with the fact that I would not be able to spontaneously construct a back story convincing enough to deal with the inevitable follow-up questions, and thus resigned myself to telling the truth.

"So…what? You a queer?"

This time my response was more forceful and immediate. Good heavens, where did *that* come from? And what implications did it hold for my doppelganger, Greg Gagne?

"I think my brother's a queer," she said.

"Isn't it past your bedtime?"

She crinkled her tiny nose. "My mom don't care."

"What about your father?"

"Aw, he's snorin' away in there. He don't know nothin'." She fell silent for several seconds and then emerged from this contemplative coma with: "He's *so* stupid that—"

"Hey, come on, now."

"—he thought a quarterback was—"

"Enough of that," I said, planting a hand on top of hers, which gripped the aluminum armrest of her lawn chair. That shut her up quite effectively, and me too.

There was a very long moment during which the words *Let's go inside* stuck in my throat; but what finally did emerge was the more ambiguous "I'm going inside."

As I reached the attic a forlorn, fading voice rose from the yard below: "You're *so* queer that…"

14. I'm Not in Love, No, No

"So Muggins, are you shit-faced?" asked Arnie, down from the Cities for a midsummer weekend.

I took inventory. "No," I concluded. "At the moment I believe I'm pie-eyed."

"I'm still just giddy, myself."

"Good God, man! Why didn't you say something?" I signaled a certified Rat's bartender to treat his affliction.[*]

Arnie drove me home around midnight. I was relieved that he did not seek a tour of the house, already so thoroughly panned by the less aesthetically fragile Nielsen on a visit the previous weekend. "Smells like somebody took a shit in here and rolled around in it," he had murmured, which I took to be his one-star rating.

On the other hand, I would have been proud to show Arnie the Arboleda girls, but there was nary an Arboleda to be found.

"They're Mexicans," I said.

---

[*] Just when we had hammered out the taxonomy of inebriation I'm not sure, but it went something like this (amounts in bottled beer): Giddy (2-3); Impaired (4-5); Pretty fucked up (6); Pie-eyed (7-9); Shit-faced (10-12); Cataleptic (N.A.); Lifeless (N.A.).

There were few public instances of catalepsy among us after our freshman year, and as of this writing no one has even once attained lifelessness. I suspect we appended these final two levels out of some submerged need to give shit-facedness a veneer of moderation. In our view of the world, to be merely shit-faced was to be perfectly capable of voting, operating heavy machinery, or teaching freshman-level English courses.

"Pardon?"

"The people in that house. They're all Mexicans."

"That's nice. What are they doing in Mankato?"

"I...I *don't know*."

There were mysteries of the Arboleda tribe that would always remain mysteries.

Mom and Dad, I assumed, had come up from Mexico. But how long ago? And why? Were all the children born there? Had they come legally? And why *Mankato*, for heaven's sake? It wasn't as if a thriving Hispanic community had been rooted here to fold them into its embrace. As far as I could tell, *they* were the Mankato Hispanic community.

And just what did Mr. Arboleda do? While an easy target for mimicry with his staggering and his monosyllabic retorts, he did keep the lot of them clothed and fed. That couldn't have been easy for him. Just having to memorize all those names would have driven a stronger parent to drink. And whatever torments compelled him to hit the bottle, he never passed that pain on to others. He ruled his clan benignly, vacantly, Ford-like.

Rosa and Laura, at least, grew less mysterious by the day. Their hobbies, so far as I could tell, were gossiping, wrestling, and collecting brothers. I had inquired early on as to how many children there were in the family and, after much finger-counting and whispered conference, received the answer "Nine, I think, counting the dead ones." Somewhere in the world, evidently, there was a Tomb of the Unknown Arboleda Sibling.

I got to know what music the girls liked, which school subjects were hard for them, which classmates they wanted dead and why. The latter theme proved a particularly fertile vein, and brought to the surface theretofore murky aspects of Rosa which, unseemly though they were, were critical to any understanding of the whole person. A fiendish sophomore gorgon named Velma figured prominently in many a tale of intrigue. Somehow, this information was important to me.

Then, in another instance of Yum Yum subculture overstaying its welcome in my life, a mop-topped high school youth named Kevin began skulking about Spring Street in the evenings. In those dark winter months, Kevin had been the dishwasher I relieved when I came in for my graveyard shift.

A sullen presence immune to my chipper greetings at the Yum Yum, he perked right up at the sight of the Arboleda girls, and they at the sight of him, and on such occasions I found that *I* became the sullen one. Kevin had better hair, dishwashing seniority, and a functioning car. How could I compete with all that?

Thus, while the girls themselves grew ever more familiar, my feelings for them—for Rosa in particular—grew into yet another mystery: What was going on here? What were my intentions? I was soon to discover that I was not the only one struggling with these very issues.

There was at least one Arboleda sibling old enough to have moved out on his own. When he came to visit, he was thronged by the adoring multitude: a sober, bright-eyed, neatly dressed poster boy for second-generation immigrant success. I didn't catch his Christian name, or if I did it was soon lost in the muddle; Mr. Arboleda was not the only man on the block with a withering cortex, not by a long shot.

One night, Arboleda Major pulled up a stump to talk. It was not a typical Arboleda encounter. The prospects of the High Flyers in their upcoming cage match did not come up even tangentially, nor did he attempt to whip me into an imaginary turnbuckle. Instead he wanted to know where I was from, how far along I was in college, what I hoped to do in life… It would dawn on me later that this might have been a preliminary interview with the Arboleda conglomerate for an entry-level position as in-law. The headhunting was subtle, with the question *Do you love Rosa?* conspicuous by its absence. And that was good, because by the end of June I would not have had a ready answer.

Without a doubt, my feelings for Rosa were more complicated than those I had had for any other girl; and it should go without saying that she aroused me, in the way that only a girl who applies the Figure-Four Leg-Lock more frequently than eye shadow can. There were nights when we two alone remained on the lawn chairs, both our houses dark and quiet, and I could have invited her up to my attic with some expectation of success—but did not, instead making that long upward trudge past the endlessly propositioning Marnie and just pretending that Rosa was with me in my lonely lair. *Oh, Rosa, I would muse on such occasions, had we but world enough and time.*

It occurred to me at times—particularly those times when Kevin came sniffing around—that if granted by some pagan deity the power to choose either claiming Rosa as my own or guaranteeing that neither Kevin nor I nor any other suitor would—not for that summer, at least—I might well have chosen the latter. It was a feeling that alarmed and bewildered me. When and wherefore had I become such a killjoy? And yet, in the privacy of my prayers, my secret mantra became *Unfuck you, Kevin*.

—◻—

As I was wrestling with my feelings for Rosa—and with Rosa herself as occasion permitted—conditions in our house were deteriorating. On the surface this would not have seemed possible. We were like some pathetic Third World capital that one already associates with famine, lawlessness, and the capricious whims of a senile dictator, now suddenly ravaged by an untreatable flesh-eating virus on top of everything else.

Our virus came first in the form of Marnie's eight-year-old son Chucky, who was suddenly staying with us indefinitely and then, with a similar lack of explanation, gone, but not before destroying my stereo headphones and slashing one of the sofa cushions.

Chucky[*] was followed hard upon by Lam, a semi-reanimated cadaver who was gracing us with his presence, I was told, because he was Cheryl's new boyfriend. This explanation overturned my assumption that he had been recruited to heal our wounded sofa via skin graft. A full week after his debut I had yet to see him either in Cheryl's company or fully detached from our only comfortable furnishing. His defining characteristic was horizontality. On my days off, however, I would begin

---

[*] One of the few names that I leave unchanged, secure in the knowledge that Chucky's cellmates have long since obviated any concern over a lawsuit. Picture, if you will, the homicidal doll of the horror franchise that would begin over a decade later, and you're seeing my Chucky. This can't be a coincidence.

to note his Lazarus-like resurrections at precisely ten a.m., opening hour for the liquor store around the corner, from whence he would return with a twelve-pack of malt liquor by five minutes past the hour, and then set about working his way through the levels up toward Catalepsy.

Lam helped himself to my Dylan eight-tracks, and that was fine. It was pleasant to have another Dylan devotee on the premises. He even did the nod-and-snort of affirmation to certain lyrics that was so common in the Dylan cult. Nothing wrong with that. It was as mundane a matter as masturbating to your high school-aged Mexican neighbors: perfectly natural and not the sort of thing one subjected to analysis—until one noticed someone doing it wrong.[*]

In Lam's case, it was an issue of timing. One does the affirming nod-and-snort after Dylan warbles some profound, trenchant utterance that non-aficionados could never hope to grasp:

You don't need a weatherman to tell which way the wind blows...

"Uh-huh." (Nod, snort)

I saw a room full of men with their hammers a-bleedin'...

"Oh, I hear that!" (Nod, snort)

...Or at least some sentiment that speaks to a personal ordeal:

I give 'er my heart but she wanted my soul...

"Aw, tell it, man!" (Nod, snort)

Lam's reactions, on the other hand, came at disconcertingly random moments.

---

[*] You want to employ brisk staccato tugs with your high school-aged Mexican neighbors; save those languid legato strokes for when you're conjuring up a dental hygienist or two.

Raspberry, strawberry, lemon and lime
What do I care?...

"Oh, *yeah*, brother!" (Nod, snort)

Don't ya tell Henry,
Apple's got your fly.

"Aw, *hell* yeah! *That's* it!" (Nod, snort)

In fairness, though, maybe he just really liked fruit.

—◻—

Lam's Dylan fetish fueled my growing insecurity around this time over my own lack of unbridled passion for music. I liked certain artists—Bowie, Dylan, Linda—but wasn't prepared to die for them the way so many of my generation seemed ready to die for their faves.

Two members of my committee of chauffeurs, Cary and Ted, for example, passed a good portion of their workday at Pearlman's locked in debates on the musical icons of the era that equaled in intensity the disputes on Scriptural interpretation between a cherubic line manager and a Baptist Vietnam vet. On any given day one could hear the Apocalypse when? question and the Robert Plant vs. Freddie Mercury issue being hashed out simultaneously in stereo.

Cary held that Ted's musical opinions were, among other things, too predictable. "Go up to Ted," he had told me, wearily, after a fruitless tussle with his antagonist, "and ask him about anybody. Doesn't matter who—the guy knows everybody going back to Mozart. He's gonna tell you exactly the same thing: Their early stuff was great, but everything they've done lately is for shit."

I found Ted in the stockroom seated on a throne he had constructed there of enormous boxes of stationery, lost in his own giddy thoughts. A gangly fellow with a classic Seventies porn moustache and enormous glasses that made his remote head look croquet ball-sized, he forever wore the expression of a man hearing the world's funniest and most profane joke mere seconds before the punch line. "Ted," I said, speaking to him for the first time—for in our society one never stooped to introducing oneself; the tacit assumption was that we all knew each other at some hive-like level of collective consciousness—"what do you make of the Eagles?"

"The Eagles? Oh, those first two albums were great," he replied, "just great. But they totally sold out with *On the Border*."

"Uh-huh. And there's this Linda Ronstadt album that I really like: *Don't Cry Now?*"

"Yeah, uh-huh, that's some good country rock," he said, as if compelled at knifepoint to make the concession. "That was her last decent record."

And so it went: Led Zeppelin? *Made something of a comeback with* Led Zeppelin IV *but blew all their credibility with that bloated piece of crap* Physical Graffiti.

Bowie? *Peaked early with* Ziggy Stardust, *been coasting ever since.*

Stevie Wonder? *Great, when he was* Little *Stevie. Shoulda stayed little.*

I thought I had him cornered with Elton John, figuring that it would pain him too much to cop to liking any part of the Elton oeuvre. Sure enough, his initial reaction was, "Oh, don't even bring that crap in here." But before I could slip away, he had added, "Gotta admit, some of his *old* radio tunes sound sorta catchy if you're messed up just right."

I had too much respect for him by that time to play the obvious trump card, John Denver, whose radio hits had proven impervious to improvement by any known combination of mood-altering substances.

And believe me, we had given those songs every chance.

Even Cary and Ted could find common ground in Alice Cooper. Thus, when the "Welcome To My Nightmare" tour came to the Cities at the end of June, tickets were acquired, and a plan quickly congealed centering on Cary's '65 Ford Galaxy. The car accommodated five, so six of us went.

We had cheap tickets in the upper tier at the Sports Arena. Alice Cooper proved to be more a theatrical act than a musical one; his stage show was designed as freaky eye candy replete with a fog machine and huge undead creatures in colorful, fuzzy costumes whom Alice would trap and decapitate with a guillotine. I couldn't help thinking of the squealing delight with which

Rosa and Laura would have greeted the spectacle.

From our seats we could see the extras backstage on break between their scenes, cradling their costume heads in their arms, slouching and smoking. It was unnerving, like watching a production of *Rosencrantz and Cookie Monster Are Dead*. Still, with a play list that included "No More Mr. Nice Guy," "Cold Ethyl," and "Only Women Bleed," it would have been hard to construct an evening more evocative of our own Zeitgeist.

The quintessentially Cooperian anthem "School's Out" certainly held special resonance for me. During its chorus, my thoughts drifted back to my recent interview with Arboleda Major. I remembered telling him that I had finished my second year of college—but that was a fudge seeing as I had failed most of my course load the last two quarters. I had "finished" the school year the same way the Vikings finished Super Bowls, not even bothering to call time-outs while the clock ran down. And there were no plans for a third year at college. Why had I bothered to, in effect, lie by omission?

After the show Cary led us bar-hopping in downtown Minneapolis. We dropped in a place called The Gay Nineties which, according to Cary's intelligence network, was not gay. A perusal of the interior, once our eyes had adjusted to the light and it was too late to back out gracefully, discredited his sources; however, a reserve of heterosexual women could be found on site, as Cary demonstrated by dancing with a few while the rest of us—even the normally irrepressible Ted—sat glued to our table *en masse* like a transplanted liver waiting for the host's antibodies to attack. On Monday we would brag about this daring urban escapade within earshot of female napkin printers to no discernible effect.

Cary dropped me off around three in the morning. Both houses were dark. Filaments of a frayed gray curtain fluttered in and out of the window of Rosa and Laura's bedroom. I crawled to the attic and drifted to sleep yet again from the bridge of that 10cc song:

Ooh, you'll wait a long time for me.
Ooh, you'll wait a long time.
I'm not in love, I'm not in love...

15. Lars Largo

Grandma died in Illinois. It was high summer and I was still without a car. Haley stepped up and volunteered his new girlfriend and her red Fiat convertible. So it was to be Val, Haley and I for the long trip to Illinois until I was found to be unteachable on a stickshift, and thus Deb—Nielsen's midlife-crisis girlfriend—was enlisted to provide another relief driver.

I had been instructed to keep an eye on Deb during those long sweltering months when Nielsen was back in Meldom for his summer job. Which I did. She was waitressing at the Gurdy and servicing at least one bartender there, probably others in a less blatant manner. I wasn't going to relate this news to Nielsen; he had instructed me only to watch, not to file reports, and I looked forward to dropping by the Gurdy once a week that summer to collect free drinks in exchange for my silence.

I liked Deb—indeed, had sniffed her bras more than once. She was elfin, smart, lean and freckly with straight butterscotch hair and rabbit teeth, and perfectly at ease with her sluttiness, though she no doubt would have assigned a different word to the trait. After her graduation the Peace Corps would dispatch her to an obscure Caribbean islet, where she no doubt spread both diseases and the knowledge for preventing them with equal ardor.

Those other three thus split seven nonstop hours driving a cramped, windblown European go-cart on two-lane roads so that I could arrive home shortly after midnight on the day of the funeral. That afternoon I saw Grandma chucked in a ditch and we were on our way back by mid-afternoon.

My friends did all that for me.

—◻—

I don't mean to give short shrift to Grandma, who had also done plenty for me; but as she had been wasting away for years there was more relief than shock associated with her passing. Though I treasured many memories of her, the one that persisted throughout the long drive was of a childhood visit when I had entered her bathroom without knocking and briefly glimpsed her naked. That image, bottled up for years, had been uncorked and pressed into service as a delaying device when I found myself under siege in Ingrid's vagina.

Obviously its efficacy was limited—no match for Ingrid, at least—but I had yet to hit on a more reliable alternative. Nielsen swore by "parents in a car accident with their heads cut off," but that had proved too harsh for my tastes. In intercourse-extending tactics as in drink, cars, and women, Nielsen favored the strong stuff.

—◻—

"Do you know what Lam did today?" asked Marnie, her fourth-grade-teacher arms akimbo, her sharp dark features scrunched into a mid-face pile-up, upon my return from the funeral.

Her posture and tone conjured eerie echoes of my mother greeting my father after yet another call from the high school principal's office. The analogy didn't quite hold, however, since my father presumably gave a shit about the answer. "He grabbed a horse," Marnie continued unbidden, "and threw it through somebody's windshield."

Now that was impressive. Like most alcoholics who take the vocation seriously, Lam tossed down a lot of liquids in the course of a day but almost no solids. He weighed a buck thirty tops. Brandishing massive ungulate mammals over his head and hurling them onto cars was not an activity one readily associated with him.

"No, no, not a *horse*," Marnie continued, testily. "One of those wooden things that Jack and Larry use."

"A sawhorse?"

"Yeah, yeah, yeah. That."

This removed the element of implausibility, yet quickly raised more questions: When? Where? Why? Whose car? What happened then? I did not ask these questions as I still lacked the pivotal shit-giving ingredient with regard to Lam's well-being, but received answers anyway: Around noon. Over there across the street. He just went nuts. Nobody knew. Somebody called the cops and they hauled him off.

The bad news: The police as well as the fire marshal would be surveiling our house now.

The good: Our sofa had been made safe for democracy.

—¤—

Now that the atmosphere at home was calmer, I could get to work on creative projects that I had long put off. This, after all, had been my rationale for quitting school: all those pesky classes, the *Reporter* column, the incessant dental checkups—they all soaked up time that I ought to have been devoting to my craft.

Finally life had been boiled down to the essentials. After an eight-hour shift at Pearlman's the evenings were all my own, as were the weekends. The attic came with a musty wicker sofa and a coffee table, perfect for setting up my portable manual typewriter and pencils and a stack of blank paper. I was all set.

I had long toyed with a concept for a comic strip called "Lars Largo, the Boneless Detective." Possessor of fierce sleuthing instincts but entirely lacking a skeleton, Lars was essentially a limp, squidlike clot of flesh, and as such entirely dependent on his faithful musclebound sidekick Frenchy to bundle him in his arms and lug him from crime scene to crime scene. When underworld masterminds were known to be laying their nefarious plots on the other side of a locked door, Frenchy would wad Lars up and sling him sidearm to the floor at such an angle that Lars would ooze through the crack, taking the evildoers by surprise.

Just how Lars, alone and boneless, was supposed to subdue his foes after that I hadn't quite worked out yet. Beyond that obstacle lay even stickier issues: I would have to master French on the fly, lest Frenchy's contributions to dialogue be forever limited to *Sacre bleu, Monsieur Largo!* Also, I couldn't draw.

Alas, Lars and Frenchy would never escape the limbo of my imagination. It was just too darned hot in that attic.

When my muse turned her back on me, I determined to better myself through the reading of Great Books: assorted Dickens, the New Testament, Shakespeare. That attempt at cultivation didn't take either. The angry heat flowing down from the roof combined with the siren call (sometimes real, sometimes imagined) of the Arboleda girls to come out and play inevitably pulled me away. And what the heck, I rationalized: Isn't the ability to skim a Frisbee off a passing Buick a creative art in its own right?

In reflective moments—and reflecting was all I had left, after failing to read and write—I thought of my friends and of what the future might hold for all of us. Someday, I knew, I *would* write; but what of the others? How would they end up? We each must choose our own path through life, our own road from cradle to grave, and my friends, true Midwestern men to the core, seemed hell-bent on competing to find the best shortcut. There was Nielsen and his drinking and driving; Durward and his drinking and poor boys; Arnie and his mescaline and cocaine. My new friend Cary had already revealed plenty of hazardous preferences: for speed, for feral women, for confrontation with superiors. For the past week, for example, he had been signing up conspirators to back him in deposing Marv as our softball manager. In the end, only Spook Blunt seemed built for the long haul. Apart from the occasional unscheduled acid trip, his worst vice was Marlboros.

I, too, enjoyed many vices but never could devote myself to them with quite as much vigor and rigor as the others—thus my smug sense of superiority. Once I finally started writing, I'd be all right. The others, though...

Or so went the old thinking. Now, however, I was forced to confront my own fatal flaw: temporizing. Abandoning my newspaper column just as I was finding a voice and a following; quitting college without even the courage to tell the registrar (or my parents); frittering away a whole summer on slow-pitch softball and forbidden Mexican fruit... *My God, what will become of me?*

Not a fortnight went by that summer without at least one long, sweaty night staring up at the attic rafters, prisoner of my own thoughts. *My God, what will become of me?*

A journal entry from that summer articulates a fear that my forty-something self was apt to show up in a time machine any day and phaser the bejesus out of me for wasting so much time. Typically, my forties came and went without my ever getting around to constructing that machine, though to this day I half expect my cranky centenarian self to pounce from behind a hedge and gum my ankles.

Come to think of it, maybe that's what the last scene of *Space Odyssey* was all about.

16. Better Softball through Chemistry

By the time Cary had browbeaten Marv into handing over the managerial reins, our team languished at the bottom of the Industrial League. Or so we had to assume, since the *Free Press* doggedly refused to acknowledge our league's existence. But it was a fairly safe bet that we were in last place, as none of our surviving members had any recollection of our ever having held even a momentary lead in any game.

Post-coup, Coach Cary named me the starting right fielder, and I immediately suffered at the plate. It wasn't the pressure: I continued to see the ball as though it were the size of a grapefruit, which it was, and to rap it as smartly as ever at middle infielders. The new factor in the equation was those middle infielders, the opposition's starters, who made an unpleasant habit of scooping up those smartly rapped balls. My line drives amounted to nothing more than Significant Momentary Annoyances, a category that included Marnie's propositions and John Denver's AM radio hits; but on such trifles the outcomes of ballgames seldom hinge.

—◻—

That summer, the delightfully unrefined Mindy and Margo from Napkinland hosted a never-ending party—a sort of Blue Earth County throwback to late-eighteenth century French salon society, only with mullets—at their apartment in the fabled Tornado Towers, a Mankato landmark that often inspired the comment

Why, look out the window, honey—it's as if someone just took a bunch of mobile homes and glued them together in stacks of four, because that is precisely what someone had done. It was the Key City's less durable answer to Stonehenge.

"How many whites do you do before a game?" Cary asked as he razored up some lines of crystal for us on our hostesses' bedroom dresser.

"I don't know—around six, usually."

"That's a lot. You might want to ratchet it down to three or so next game," he said. "That way you'll be more fluid at the plate, not so jerky."

You want to talk jerky, let's discuss your dancing technique, I wanted to whine. But Cary had invited me into the girls' bedroom to privately share these home truths with me, as well as his crystal, so I bore the criticism manfully.

"Have a beer before the game, too, to take the edge off. And pot's okay, too, but only one or two hits."

"Yeah, yeah. I'll think about it," I moped, dutifully snorting my lines. Then I rummaged through a dresser drawer and found a bra to sniff while Cary set up lines for himself.

"Having fun?" he sneered.

"You're just jealous because you don't have a fetish of your own."

"Shouldn't you sniff panties?" he asked between toots.

"Don't be so cliché."

"How about getting somebody to spank you?"

"Spanking's taken," I muttered, lustily snuffling a cup.

Judging from the size, the garment had to be Mindy's, though I would have been just as pleased with one of Margo's. I was an equal opportunity bra sniffer.

"So… Is it getting you horny?"

"Hard to tell."

"Maybe you should look for some *dirty* bras to sniff."

"Why? What would they smell like?"

"Shit, I dunno," he said with some irritation. "Sweat, maybe."

That gave me pause. "*Do* they sweat?"

"Who? Girls?"

"Tits, I mean."

"How the hell should I know?"

He knew. He had to know. He just didn't want to tell me. I craved the means to bind him and torture him until he talked.

"What does that one smell like?" he asked.

"Oxydol."

"Okay. So, you about done, then?"

"Yeah."

"'S go grab some beers before they're gone."

"M'kay."

—¤—

Needless to say, Cary's advice about my pregame regimen was genius. A week or so later, our chemical trials began to yield results, and here is where the montage set to a rousing Kenny Loggins anthem would commence in the mid-Eighties biopic of my Industrial League career:

Kato Engineering game: One for four, on base twice with a hit and an error, one run scored in a 7-5 come-from-behind win.

Hiniker Cab: Two for five plus a bona fide right-field putout in a 5-3 victory.

Beautz Dodge Dealership: Two for four with that rarest of slow-pitch oddities, a base on balls. We were getting cocky now and gleefully baited the hapless opposing pitcher into a meltdown in a 9-3 triumph, not even as close as the score implied.

Next up: Chesney Auto Parts. My strategy was two-pronged. I threw a little dab of strawberry mescaline into my personal pregame spread. And since I was down to my last thirty or so white cross anyway, I resolved to distribute them among like-minded teammates.

I greeted them Welcome Wagon-style as they stepped out of their cars at the windswept diamond in the North Mankato hilltop area. A few for Coach Cary, a few for Woodie, a few for Fast Eddie.

I wavered in Hoppy's case. Forcing amphetamines on a shy and chubby chain smoker felt like pouring the proverbial gasoline on the proverbial fire, but as I saw it we all had to sacrifice for the team. In the end, I gave him just enough speed to shorten his life by about a week. He was probably fated to spend those final days lying around in agony at some hospice anyway, so in effect I was doing him a favor.

On the first pitch of my first at-bat I walloped the ball over the head of the left fielder, who had offended me by playing shallow. For once, instead of frantically lunging for every base I could get, I broke into a home run trot. It felt nice—majestic even—not unlike wafting to earth from an airplane. I could get used to home run trotting.

Meanwhile, the ball had been retrieved and relayed to the rover-back. Still, I paid no heed to the frantic yips and flapping paws of the Chihuahua-headed martinets who had until recently been my teammates, and trotted casually across home plate, narrowly beating the catcher's tag.

It was just as I had always said: All I needed was playing time.

17. Okay, It Was a Shoe

I fell in love with Cary that summer. He was so devoted to my softball career. He was, as Yogi Berra once said, learning me his experience. I was sure that he could learn me much about the ballgame of life, as well.

Cary knew where all the best parties with the most accessible women could be found, and kindly took me along with him to those parties so that I could stand around and watch him seduce those women.

The lessons did not take. I didn't get it; still don't. Cary was tall and rock-star slim, to be sure, but the pale skin that is the hallmark of redheads tended to make his outbursts of acne that much more conspicuous, and his dancing was, as noted earlier, even jerkier and more flagrantly Caucasoid than my own. Surely some of Cary's sideways-lurching, elbow-flailing moves on the dance floor were, in the words of perpetually outraged AWA ringside announcer Roger Kent, *banned in some states and should be in this one*. Even when not dancing Cary tended to fidget and squirm like an eight-year-old in an outgrown suit enduring an hour-long Easter sermon.

In a typical party situation, he would fidget and squirm his way up to a couple of unknown females, flap his arms stiffly at his sides (his signature move, suggesting an aw-shucks affability) and greet them with a droll *bon mot* along the lines of "So what are you girls up to tonight?," which would be ignored, and yet, unfazed, he would renew the attack with the always uproarious "You havin' a good time?," which they would likewise ignore, by now exchanging derisive whispers behind their palms. Then he would address himself specifically to the more achievable of the two:

"Hey, look. I'm just tryin' to be affable here. Why do you have to be such a total bitch?"

"Excuse me?"

"Just wanted to know if you were havin' a good time is all."

"Well, we *were* until *you* showed up."

"Hey, look. I'm sorry [*stiff arm flap*]. I didn't mean to yell at you like that."

"Well…that's all right."

"You wanna dance?"

And ten minutes of jerky elbow-flailing later he was leading Achievable Girl out the door of whoever's house we were in while I leaned slack-jawed against the kitchen counter, as cowed as a hunter-gatherer recoiling in the glow of an anthropologist's Bic lighter.

To recap: He accosted unknown females who had offered no hint of seeking his society. He crudely, sharply insulted one of them. Then he danced badly with her, and soon after led her out to his car. Following this logic, I ought to have been madly in love with Red. I wasn't sure I wanted to go on living in a world that made so little sense. Watching Cary operate afforded the likes of me a rare chance to comprehend the vastness of my own ignorance, and I was not grateful for it.

Cary returned half an hour later. I braced myself for the inevitable envy-provoking description of the encounter in the car. Even if there had been nothing more than sloppy kissing and groping, it would have constituted more such recreation than I had enjoyed in this arid post-Ingrid era, and the length of his absence suggested that more than that had transpired.

In the meantime I had been mulling derogatory remarks to make about that shameless concubine Achievable Girl so as to devalue whatever form of gratification she had bestowed; but then, as he always did, Cary outfoxed me by offering no commentary whatsoever, which infuriated me all the more. Something significant must have transpired, though, because he was uncommonly passive and unfidgety for a while, content to sit on the sidelines and sip his beer as we watched a halter-topped Amazon limbo and writhe in the living room.

"Oh, yeah," I whispered in the hushed, pan-cultural tone of horny, cowardly men the world over. "This funky-backed chick just put my spine outta place."

"'Funky *black* chick,'" Cary corrected.

"Are you sure? I could've sworn it was 'funky-backed chick'."

"Think about it," he said, pausing for a slow sip. "Why would just her *back* be funky?"

"You've got a point there."

"I'm sure it's 'funky *black* chick.' Bowie has a thing for black chicks."

"But this chick here isn't black."

"You'll just have to come up with a new lyric to quote, then, won't you?"

But by the time I did, she was gone.[*]

—◻—

There would be other parties that summer, of course, with other funky and/or mellow chicks for me to fail to approach until it was too late. There would be after-bar parties, birthday parties, napkin-printer parties, pre-concert parties, post-game parties, notorious parties at some mysterious guy's apartment upstairs from the South Street Saloon. Parties for the planning of other parties.

The next weekend, I would sniff Deb's bras anew at her birthday party. The fetish still wasn't paying dividends. In Deb's case, it lacked even the thrilling fear of exposure, since she had granted me free access to her dresser weeks earlier. I knew I just had to give it time, though. All great fetishes are the evolutionary product of trial and error, and someday I would be hailed by a generation of mouth-breathers yet unborn as the Father of Bra Sniffing. History offers far less auspicious fates.

"You gotta go see this movie, Muggins. It's fuckin' intense," Nielsen related between swigs of Miller, while I sniffed away and wondered if I dared asked him whether boobs sweated or not. "This high school kid next to Deb

---

[*] For the record, it's "this *mellow* black chick."

had his fingers over his eyes the whole time. And there's this one part where this guy's scuba diving at night under this boat, see—and *a fuckin' guy's head comes floating through the bottom of the boat!* The kid goes, 'That was a shoe, right? *Tell me that was a shoe!'*

"Great shit," he said, concluding his review.

The party was hosted by Deb herself and her James Court roommates, a lineup now consisting of Val and one Helen Gronky, locally famous Teutonic blond heiress to a farm-implement dealership in a nearby town and the providential product of Deb's roommate search. Arnie called her Helen of Waterville, the Face that Launched a Thousand Tractors.

Helen was uncommonly chaste by the standards of Mankato in that era and far more so by the standards of Deb's apartment. Hoppy had managed to date her a few times the year before and described a brief foray to second base, a claim that inspired noisy cynicism over lunch at the Hofbrau Haus one day until I expressed how much I'd like to give *her* bra one thorough sniffing if ya know what I mean, heh-heh, thereby summarily quashing all discourse for the duration of lunch break.

Deb could not serve us Helen of Waterville, alas, but was otherwise the perfect hostess for her own birthday bash, laying out a spread that included magic mushrooms and Thai stick and other assorted delicacies scrounged from her myriad summer flings, the consumption of which led inexorably to mass skinny dipping in the James Court pool. Helen came out with us but did not skinny dip, thus forever denying me the chance to slip in a pretentious "topless towers of Ilium" reference.[*]

In spite of a mood much enhanced by Deb's appetizers, I skinny-dipped only with reluctance. I was not comfortable with my own nude form in public. The thing is, I just felt that there was too much, well, *business* down there. I wished I'd been properly circumcised at birth as everyone else seemed to have been.

I stuck close to the edge of the pool or made timid sprints from side to side, careful to expose only my less offensive rear view. Meanwhile

---

[*] Though I just did anyway.

Arnie, floating blithely on his back in the deep end with five mood-altering substances coursing through his bloodstream and his stubby little periscope up, mused, "Geez, you guys, if we died right now, it would be, like, *perfect*." Easy for him to say, the circumcised bastard.

—¤—

Durward confided to me that night that he was going to make a run at Helen as soon as he, Arnie, and Nielsen got settled into their own James Court unit in the fall, and I told him that was tits, just tits. I could tell by the reverent, hushed way he pronounced her name that he was smitten; later, after the inevitable rejection and/or humiliation, would come Helen's demotion to "that concubine" and the filthy poem in her honor.

We conferred on the Helen issue in the dusty recesses of my attic where, in desperation, he ended up crashing. He proved a model houseguest in that he did not pleasure himself in my presence over the lingering images of Helen, or else did so with preternatural deftness. But if he refrained on my account it was a shame, for he was soon to be deprived of the capacity for inspiration for at least a week.

The next morning we were obstructed in our descent to the main floor by the sprawled pentagonal form of Marnie on the stairway landing. She had tumbled there an hour earlier, immobilizing herself. Her badly wrenched knee had turned the color of rotten plums. Durward and I each shouldered a jiggly arm and lugged her to the sofa.

"I gotta get to the hospital," Marnie croaked, and she was right. We were fortunate enough to have a large hospital just around the corner on Fourth Street as well as easy access to Durward's full-size GMC pickup, which had more than once stood the test of hauling dead stock on the Roe Ranch that summer, so we were good to go.

"Can you go get me a clean shirt?" Marnie asked.

To this I heard the phantomy voice of my similarly jiggle-bag-armed real-life fourth-grade teacher answering *Can I? I don't know, Marnie. Am I able?* But I dutifully went up and retrieved a shirt from her dresser. I ignored her bras; I had my standards.

I came back downstairs determined not to let my line of sight fall upon Marnie because I had lived with her long enough to know the consequences. Durward, alas, did not know them, and had already been turned to stone. I tossed the shirt in Marnie's general direction. A minute later, we helped her lunge onto the bed of the truck and soon had her signed in at the emergency room. A mere shadow of his former self all this while, Durward drove in silence. Only after we had arrived at the Happy Chef for an early lunch did he begin to unburden himself.

"Josh, she…she took off her shirt. She…"

"I know, Dur, I know."

"…didn't warn me. She just…took it *off*."

"You'll get over it. Trust me."

"Right in *front* of me."

I counseled him to dwell on happy things—circus clowns, fishing with his dad, Christmas mornings. Raindrops on roses. It was useless.

"She wasn't wearin' nothin' under it, Josh!"

I was at a loss. I led him to the Happy Chef statue outside and pressed the button that activated the Chef's voice, hoping that the familiar tone would soothe him[*], but it soon became apparent that this spiritual approach wasn't helping. Next, I tried warming up some leftover Thai stick and plugging an Edgar Winter tape into his truck's eight-track player, to better effect.

Herein lay the great advantage of living in the age of Sex, Drugs, and Rock-and-Roll: even lads like Durward and me could always gain quick access to two out of three, which made our travails with that other, more elusive item a tad easier to bear.

---

[*] In theory the Chefolith spouted humorous, food-related remarks aimed at youngsters, but time and weather had eroded its internal recording to the point of scratchy incomprehensibility, and trying to decipher its oracular pronouncements was a post-closing-time ritual of long standing. Depending on one's state of mind, the Chef might emit a jaunty version of *The sow is mine now, Karras, you faithless slime* or *Paul is dead—mourn him, mourn him.*

18. Vengeance Is Mine

After what came to be known as the Chesney Methedrine Massacre we went on to finish the season with a record of six and six, but still had one more score to even. I home-run-trotted up to Ted Wexler, captain of a splinter Pearlman's Industrial League team, the following day to ask if his squad had encountered the sheet metal workers yet.

"Yeah, yeah. We just played them."

"Have any trouble with their first baseman?"

"Big guy? Red beard, big mouth?" he asked.

"That's the guy."

"What an asshole."

"We played them first game of the season."

"That dickhead wouldn't let up on us *the whole game*."

"Hey, you should have heard his early stuff."

At two p.m. on Saturday under lowering skies, we stood behind the third base line at the hilltop diamond, backing up our new friends from Chesney Auto Parts. Word of our plan had gotten around; I gave up trying to count heads at forty.

Along the opposite base line the sheet metal workers had set up their now familiar accouterments: two massive coolers full of encouragement and lawn chairs for the Hutt-like beings that the players, in moments of even poorer than usual judgment, had married. Even on such a balmy late-summer day as this, the sheet metal wives conjured up the image of thick Christmas candles melting ever so slowly into the synthetic fabric of their lawn chairs. The *unfuck you* curse might have been received as a blessing by all concerned in that crowd.

Their leadoff man doubled, then stood still for two outs. Now the cleanup hitter stepped to the plate. Our placards went up and a cry never before heard at an Industrial League slow-pitch game arose:

DOWN…WITH…RED!… DOWN…WITH…RED!…

Red glanced over, more curious than offended, and slowly perused our signs:

DEATH TO RED!

GO BACK TO RUSSIA! YOU COMMIE BASTARD!

WHO'S A HAT SHITTER <u>NOW</u>?

BETTER DEAD THAN RED!

By now he was officially more offended than curious, for if there is anything a man of Red's breeding cannot abide it is a reading assignment, especially in the middle of an at-bat. But class was only beginning.

We waved our placards during every Red plate appearance. We jeered when he faced an incoming throw at first and cheered when he bobbled the ball. Our enthusiasm hardly flagged when, clearly flustered, he tried to take cover behind his teammates along the sideline. *"That's right! Have another beer, you fat pig!"* bellowed Hoppy, stunning the rest of us into silence by stepping so violently out of character. Mental note: no more free pregame crank for Hoppy.

Mrs. Red's hatred for us burned through her red-rimmed cat's-eye sunglasses so fiercely that the backfire from it seemed to weld her even more indissolubly to her lawn chair. If she could not stand by her man, at least she would slouch by him. Red's teammates, though, were tellingly loath to stick up for him. When their third baseman had to waddle into our midst in pursuit of a foul pop-up, we politely parted to let him pass. The play made, he jogged back into position without so much as a "Smart-ass college punks…" under his breath.

From our side, though, the torrent of abuse would stream forth without pause until the final out, which came all too soon in the middle of the fifth after a big Chesney rally brought the Mercy Rule into effect.

Ted and I concurred that the first annual Hate Red Day had come off smashingly. No one should go home a loser on such a festive occasion, we felt, so we resolved to walk across the field and offer Red a cold Pabst.

"What? *Fuck you, you assholes!*"

His brand loyalty to Schlitz was touching.

"Oh, come on, Red. We were just having some fun," said Ted.

"Oh, *fun??* With all them signs and all that a-raisin' a ruckus?," he said, jabbing a calloused index finger at our matching *Death to Red* t-shirts—and that creamy liddle index finger was *a-shakin'!* "Well, let me tell *you* somethin'—I ain't *ever* seen nothin' like *that* before. Hell, you don't even see that sorta thing at a *Twins* game! You hear me?"

A-shudderin' with fury, he turned to dismiss us, then pivoted to add, superfluously, "Not even at a *Twins* game!" And with that he waddled out of our lives forever, granting us one final glimpse of his broad, unkissed caboose.

19. Later, Alligator

Meanwhile, back in Meldom, a suitable donor had finally been found for the Missile's long-awaited cookies transplant.

"Hey, she sounds good to me," Nielsen chirped over the roar of the engine.

Though not qualified to give a professional opinion, I agreed that it was a sound that lifted spirits even here in this dank and acrid motorhead den.

"While yer in town, why'ncha stop at the Legion for a barley pop or two? I'll get hold of Durward."

"I don't want to risk driving the Missile back drunk after dark."

"Well, all right, then. Hey—you flaccid?"

"Pretty much."

"Just checkin'."

—¤—

Back home by mid-afternoon, I was enjoying an eerie silence on the sofa when Marnie hobbled into the living room and said, "You wanna come out back and help us pick up Lam?"

Ah, yes, Lam. His absence from the sofa accounted for aforesaid eerie silence. Some days earlier authorities had released Lam—according to Lam—"on my own recognizance," a move that struck longtime Lam observers as a bold gambit on the part of said authorities given Lam's fickle capacity for recognizing himself. I would not have wagered heavily on Lam's successfully picking himself out of a lineup that consisted of Aretha Franklin, Lam, and a half-loaded caulking gun. In any case he was back, and had promptly resumed his idealistic, solitary revolt against arbitrary societal restrictions on the consumption of malt beverages before noon.

"What happened to Lam?" I asked.

"Cheryl finally got fed up with him and threw him off the fire escape."

"We have a fire escape?"

We found Lam in our small barren back yard, moaning and writhing like an ant beneath the magnifying glass of a giant, malicious child. A gash at his temple gave the lie to Alice Cooper's recent assertion that only women bleed. Cheryl hovered about, apologizing and fawning over him to the extent that a three-hundred-pound woman can be said to fawn.

I took a minute to look around, having never been out here. Sure enough, there was a steep, rickety staircase leading up to a second floor door, which, I grasped, was concealed on the inside by a tattered red tapestry. In classic Spring Street fashion, our fire escape was both impossible to find and eminently flammable.

Looking to my right, I noted that the back end of the corner liquor store abutted our property line. I mentioned that from where Lam writhed he was only a rotten wooden fence, a thick coat of ivy and a solid brick wall from a Paradise Regained of whiskey, vodka and ice-cold malt liquor. Even with bruised ribs and a sprained ankle he seemed willing to make a go of it, which helped us raise him up.

We dragged Lam through the kitchen and poured him into his conventional sprawl across the sofa just as Bob Dylan rasped:

The machine guns are roaring
The puppets heave rocks

...to which he nodded and snorted, signifying to us that he would be all right.

For me, this was the moment at which Reality slapped me upside the head, at which the glamour of living in Mankato society—at least the Spring Street chapter of it—began to peel away, and at which I resolved to move on. For one thing, there was far too much hurling going on around here. If people weren't hurling sawhorses through windshields, they were hurling sawhorse hurlers off fire escapes. I'm a lover, not a hurler. The poor we will always have with us: so Jesus taught. Duly noted, but he didn't say anything about ceding them all our sofa space or letting them mess with our eight-tracks. Enough was enough.

The return of the Missile allowed house-hunting with Haley to begin in earnest. For his part, Haley had finally abandoned his quest to make his home even more uninhabitable than it had been when he had moved in. Miraculously, he recovered most of his damage deposit from his slumlord, who had been humbled by Hedley G. Stonebridge's brilliant photojournalistic masterpiece. A few weeks later I signed a lease on a unit in a trailer park on 14 East, down the road from the Chef.

Young Kevin was on hand again the last night I resided in the Spring Street house, and I suppose that it was the threat posed by his presence that moved me to action.

"We oughtta go cruising," Laura had said.

"Yeah, sure," Kevin had then murmured, stamping out a butt and reaching for his keys.

"I wanna go in Josh's car," Rosa then remarked.

"Well, all right."

"Shotgun!"

I had never really wanted to marry A Girl Just Like the Girl (so the old song goes) Who Married Dear Old Dad. On the other hand, my embryonic marriage fantasies were equally devoid of girls who aggressively called shotgun.

All the same, I was proud to have Rosa in the bucket seat beside me for the first time as I revved the engine to life. I did not forget about the naïve and coltish Laura, however: I adjusted the rearview so as to make sure Kevin kept his dishpan hands to himself back there.

And soon we four were promenading on the hilltop strip past fast-food franchises, the Yum Yum and the Super America as the sly, beaming Chef spooned his beneficence upon us. My left arm dangled oh so nonchalantly out my window while the girls jabbered so fast they might as well have been speaking Spanish, something that (it suddenly occurred to me) I had never heard them do.

Occasionally a predatory vehicle of some species or other would drift into the left lane, growl a mufflerless growl at us and then squeal away in a foul, gray cloud of burnt rubber and ancient oil. *Money just laying on the road,* my high school driver's ed teacher would have lamented. I rolled my eyes to indicate how far beneath my dignity it was to respond in kind to such behavior, then turned and rolled my eyes again for those in the back seat who had missed it the first time.

In my mind, the progressive sounds of the Eagles and Electric Light Orchestra had vanished from the radio, replaced by the Diamonds crooning "Little Darlin'" in falsetto harmony. I suddenly ached to slick my hair into a pompadour with Dax Grease and don a tight white t-shirt and roll a pack of Camels into the sleeve like the noble drag racer in *American Graffiti.*

"Lookit!" cried Rosa suddenly. "See that Camaro? I saw that guy kick the shit out of this one guy one time at the Kato Ballroom."

"No shit?" said Kevin.

"You've been to the *Kato Ballroom?*" I heard myself yelp, like a lapdog backing into a knitting needle.

"Yeah, sure," said Rosa. "What's the big deal, man?"

Don't call me "man," I wanted to squeal, on the brink of a seizure. "But... but they serve drinks, don't they?"

"No," she said, "not *in* the ballroom."

"How can you go to a place like that? Does your mom know you go up there?"

"Yeah, sure," she said, facing away.

In truth, all I knew of the Kato Ballroom was that it stood somewhere off Third Avenue, an ominous, obscure artery that flowed like a black hole into some hidden Fifth-Dimension Mankato where dinosaurs roamed the earth. Some sinister, quasi-Iranian band called Shah-Allah-Shah or some such thing played dance music there, or so the radio told me. Most alarming of all, the Third Avenue region was too remote to be accessed on foot. Surely someone had *driven* Rosa to that Concubine of Babylon, the Kato Ballroom.

"What on earth do you *do* there?"

"You know… Just hang out," she replied, visibly bristling. You could actually count her bristles.

"Well, *Laura* would never go to a place like that," I clucked. "Would you, Laura."

A leaden silence followed.

"Would you, Laura?"

"What," Rosa interjected, "is the big deal with the Kato Ballroom?"

"It's just—you guys are so young and…" The only word I could think of was *nubile*, which I elected to leave unspoken.

"Have *you* ever been there?" Rosa sneered, seizing the offensive.

"No."

"Do you even know where the fuck it is?"

"*Hey!* Language, *language!*"

"Oh, look up ahead! It's Velma's piece-a-shit car," said Rosa, ignoring my admonition. "Pull up next to 'em!"

No longer the captain of my soul, let alone my car, I obliged. Now Rosa was dangling out the window so precariously that Kevin felt compelled to slip a finger through a loop of her jeans in order to stabilize her. I wanted to slap his wrist and tell him that if there were any belt-loop-hooking to be done around here I was perfectly capable of handling it myself, but at that moment I was too afraid that we would end up one cranky Mexican teen short if he relaxed his grip. I realized at that instant that if indeed we were going to cast a remake of *American Graffiti*, Kevin would be the cool hot-rodder; I'd be the geek who ends up going MIA in Nam.

Now someone outside my car who sounded suspiciously like my naïve and unsullied neighbor was screeching, "Hey, *eat me*, you *bitt-chessss!* Yeah, *you! E-e-e-at me-e-e!*" right there in the presence of Laura and God Almighty and the Happy Chef.

Summer of Marv

I was simultaneously appalled by her manners and spellbound by the expanding view of Latina butt cleavage, a rarer treat in Mankato in those days than good Mexican cuisine. There followed a cacophony of honking and mightily displeased voices of indeterminate gender. "Oh, *yeah?*" screeched Rosa, "Velma, you're so *fat,* your *pant size* is—" But the insult—a fairly good one at that—was broken off as Rosa retracted herself back into the car, middle fingers of both hands still frozen upright, and said, "*Shit,* Josh, *stomp on it!* They're comin' *after* us!"

—◻—

After the move to the trailer I would occasionally return to Spring Street to check for mail, even though the forwarding address form had long ago been filed at the PO. With the end of summer came the end of lawn society, however, so there began to be less and less chance of running into the girls.

Jack and Larry had finally completed the far wall of the Arboleda house, just as the opposite side—painted months before—had begun to peel. "Life itself is like a too slowly painted house," I muttered aloud, and then tried to make that good somehow.

I kept finding excuses to drive by there all through the winter. A family with small children eventually took over and refurbished my house, which must have discombobulated poor Lam no end. The following year I drifted out East.

I came back, of course—the adage that there is no passion like that of a convert holds just as true for poseur Minnesotans as for fundamentalist zealots—back to school and back to my *Reporter* column.

Four years later I found myself in the lobby of the Burton Hotel with my editor shortly before midnight on a plutonian shore Monday in late January. I was four months from graduation and thence departure to the Far East, where off-and-on dabbling in journalism would segue into a university position and later a side career producing volumes of self-involved personal writings.

Whenever we went over deadline on a *Reporter* edition, the Burton was where we took our proofs to be rushed off to Rochester or Albert Lea or Pluto—wherever it was they went. While my editor railed at an uncomprehending new desk clerk, I wandered through the interior passageway that led to the hotel pub, Brannigan's.

It was a redneck establishment that I had never patronized, nor had any intention of patronizing now. But the Burton lobby was still infested with those creepy old men. The bloom was off my rose now; I was as old as Hedley G. Stonebridge had been when he used to unnerve me, and, though still in denial over it, already losing my hair. Even so, the lobby-mummies did not discriminate. Some appeared to be among the same lost souls who had scoped out the denim-cutoffs-clad butts of Cary, Ted, Hoppy and me whenever we had steamed past them en route to the lunch-hour buffet at Harry's Hofbrau Haus way back in the Summer of Marv.

Brannigan's was squalid; but at least it was a bar, with the warm and homey aroma that a neighborhood pub should offer on a Monday evening—that of salty nuts and stale beer—with the undulating murmur of mildly soused early-in-the-week chatter and Waylon Jennings on the Wurlitzer. Its quintessentially Irish name implied pugnacity and brawls, but there seemed little danger of violence tonight, with every patron's pulse slowed to a hibernal crawl.

Most of these denizens huddled in padded booths with wooden backs so high that the booths could almost have been called cubicles, so that the periodic blasts of subzero air from the front door could only obliquely strike them. A few ragged souls who really did wish to drink themselves to death clung to unsheltered outposts along the bar.

The bartender ignored me, which was fine. I just wanted a few minutes of warmth and atmosphere. The place conjured memories of the late, lamented Rathskeller, gone to its reward three summers before—if only in the same way that every young woman conjures a lonely old man's memories of his long-lost first love. Soon my eyes were drawn to a booth where a burly, feral brute glared across the table at a party unseen. He reminded me of Chad, my old line manager from Pearlman's—had the same Lon-Chaney-in-mid-transformation vibe going for him—but with a more authentic viciousness. Not even fast-pitch softball could slake his thirst; for his species, it was blood sports or no sports at all. I felt sympathy for his unseen companion, the recipient of his scowls and snarls, even before a shift in posture brought a curtain of shimmering black hair into view.

Without thinking I stepped forward and said, "Rosa?"

The effect on both parties in the booth was electric. Expressions of confusion and recognition flickered in quick succession across the garishly painted face of someone I used to know, followed by a stare of haunted helplessness. Meanwhile, her escort began to emit a low, rumbling growl reminiscent of a certain male Doberman with whom I had been roommates a few years earlier. This was not immediately alarming even to a congenital coward like me; that Doberman had turned out to be all talk and no action.

I longed to probe Rosa's views on the still recent triumph of the High Flyers over Blackjack Lanza and Bobby Heenan, to learn what she made of new figures like the Iron Sheik and the Mongolian Stomper. And how was Laura? Had she grown up as pretty as expected? And what had become of Kevin? With the alternative so starkly on display, the notion of Rosa ending up with Kevin suddenly seemed a thing devoutly to be wished. So many questions percolated in my overworked, overcooked brain.

But the snarling persisted, and with male Dobermans one isn't likely to get lucky twice in a row. Those odds now occurred to me, and since nobody was inviting me to stay I did what came naturally to me, then and now, in such tense situations: I fled.

A blast of impossibly frigid air gripped me as I stepped outdoors, searing my lungs and fast-freezing the lining of my nostrils. One of my classes that term was a world literature survey course. I recalled how Hell, in Dante's vision, also grew colder, not warmer, when one neared its most hopeless depths.

20. A Little Off the Top

Meanwhile, down at James Court Apartments, at the bottom of Stadium Road's precipitous slope, Arnie, with smarmy ruthlessness, had badgered Durward into helping him decorate their groovy new ground-floor two-bedroom pad. Sentences the likes of which had never penetrated Durward's ears throughout his upbringing on the Roe Ranch—"See, if we slide the coffee table a skosh over this way, it opens up this natural *flow*"—were stunning him into an automaton-like subservience.

It was heartwarming to see those two working in harness, regardless of how far apart their motives lay. Arnie's goal was clearly art for art's sake, his crowning achievement being the construction of an understated retro bookshelf from old wooden milk crates and fence rails and other found objects of similar rusticity salvaged from the Roe Ranch. It was a homey, homely structure that soon housed their stereo, combined record collections, and, for appearances, some prop books.

To Durward the concepts of open space and natural flow were inextricably linked with his hopes for at long last engaging a willing partner in the Wheelbarrow, his favorite hypothetical sexual position, which had never been feasible in a cramped dorm room. The carpeted living room at James Court now provided him ample space in which at least to pantomime the act, often with the less than voluntary assistance of Arnie's dog.[*]

---

[*] It's said that every generation believes itself to be the one that invented sex. I for one never suffered such delusions on behalf of my generation, but for God's sake at the very least I thought that we had invented the Wheelbarrow. Imagine my chagrin years later upon learning that we hadn't.

—◻—

We didn't go in for that hoity-toity stuff out at the trailer park.

For one thing, the smaller bedroom at the trailer, to which I had condemned Haley by virtue of having found the trailer and moved in first, was too small even to visualize doing the Wheelbarrow in; but that didn't stop him from having loud sex with Val, an ostentatious alto howler, and that got old quickly; on the other hand, Haley did not nod and snort to any type of music; he neither hurled large objects nor was himself hurled by others; and never once did he cajole me to lie down with him "just for a minute" when I got up at night to use the bathroom.

Plus he could cook, and often had good weed to offer as an appetizer, though never very much of it. When the supply ran low we drove across town to James Court, where they had quantity sans quality. Durward's summer science project on the Roe Ranch had borne fruit. After nurturing his patch of marijuana plants through an August drought he had reaped the first crop of RoeWeed™, and, much as Pa Ingalls used to do in a bygone era, proudly brought his produce to market in Mankato in several thirty-three-gallon Hefty bags.

It was pleasant no longer having to worry about running out, especially in that it took an inordinate amount of RoeWeed™ to effect any change in one's attitude—on top of which there was the product's rather unfortunate tendency to explode, so that we soon abandoned attempts to consume it in the form of joints. By the seventh or eighth round of bong hits, asphyxiation could not be ruled out as the primary cause of the light-headedness that set in. One might achieve the same result with less trouble by buttoning up a very tight shirt.

Arnie didn't care much for the smoke; was willing, in fact, to risk conviction (if indeed RoeWeed™ were proved at trial to be a controlled substance) by releasing the fumes through the sliding doors that opened onto a small concrete patio and a well-tended wooded lawn that sloped down toward the parking lot. His black Labrador, Frances, no longer the fugitive she had been in the dorm, could run free here and draw gasping *Whooaaaaa!*s from oxygen-starved guests with her spectacular Frisbee-snagging leaps.

It quickly became clear that no detail of apartment upkeep would escape Arnie's notice. The frequency of dishwashing and the technique with which it was performed; the sorting of soiled clothes and the manner of laundering them; the choice of music on the stereo when company was present[*]; the choice of alcoholic beverages to stock and the proper way to array them on the countertop or inside the refrigerator—all the minutiae of daily life were subject to his whimsy, and by controlling their environment he steadily made Nielsen and Durward—in the phrase of a later, cruder generation—his bitches. Any act that was left undone or performed in a less than fastidious manner drew not a tantrum but a weary, disdainful chuckle that felt infinitely worse to the reprobate. One never angered Arnie; one merely let him down.

The Meldom pair bore these tyrannies with remarkable patience most of the time, even admitting that Arnie's meticulousness was "good for" them, although there were to be those occasions when Arnie might come home to find his roommates trying to stuff his dog headfirst into the oven. Frances was to be the inadvertent instrument of many petty acts of rebellion, most notably when Durward brought home a half dozen leftover bean burritos from his cafeteria job and secretly force-fed them to the animal just before Arnie was to shut her in his room with him for the night.

—◻—

Meanwhile, back at Pearlman Printing, full-time status became somewhat less glamorous when nearly all my colleagues went back to half-day shifts to accommodate their fall schedules at MSC.[†] Conditions were made that much

---

[*] Or even when company wasn't. You just didn't throw any old thing on the turntable simply because you wanted to hear it. There were specific genres to be enjoyed in the morning, in the afternoon, and before bedtime; there were tunes that suited, respectively, occasions of celebration, despair, frustration, trepidation, pique, and still finer shades of human emotion the existence of which the rest of us had not suspected; there were artists specifically designated for listening to during every conceivable pattern of weather; and so it went.

[†] Which, it should be duly noted, had metamorphosed over the summer into MSU for reasons we never quite grasped.

lonelier by a falling out I'd had with Coach Cary.

Over lunch one day at the Hofbrau Haus, the proper definition of "having sex" had ignited a debate that uncannily foreshadowed a somewhat higher profile discussion on that very topic at the top echelons of American government two decades later. Cary trail-blazed a future president's position that only genital intercourse counted. Handjobs were not even on the table as far as he was concerned, and even oral sex was not "sex." "It is *not,*" he said, in a brief summation speech.

In my "Is *so*" rebuttal, I staked out territory for a future special prosecutor by proposing the definition of sex to be "any action involving more than one party that results directly in an orgasm for at least one of those parties, preferably me." It was that cut and dried as I saw it. My career stats hadn't budged since May, and Cary's nefarious attempt to rewrite the rule book posed the greatest threat to my tenuous claim to a sex life since the unveiling of *unfuck you.*

And so the days floated by with a drab sameness, and nights remained sexless (by either party's definition) with no likely girlfriend prospects on the horizon. An idle penis is the devil's playground, I'd heard said. As long as I wasn't using the darned thing, I figured I might as well have it cut.

—◻—

Not cut off completely, of course. I wasn't that frustrated yet. On the contrary, I was very much embracing life, if not women—had even driven up to St. Paul earlier that month for a clandestine meeting with a shadowy character who called himself "Dr. Lay."[*]

Now, on a gorgeous Wednesday in mid-September, I took a personal leave day from Pearlman's to drive up for my second visit. In the OR, a little curtain was set up across my stomach just below the ribcage to prevent me from viewing the unspeakable carnage about to take place backstage.

"I'm injecting the local anesthesia now," said a nurse who reminded me of a beloved aunt back in Illinois. "This is going to sting a little." If I were

---

[*] Presumably because it was his name.

in her line of work, I'd probably tell patients, *I'm going to give you a little prick.* *Ha-ha! Get it? A little prick!!* But that's just me.

In scarcely over a minute, about the time it usually took me to complete a sex act, a disturbing numbness set in, as if my prized possession were no longer there at all. At any moment I imagined the little curtain might rise to reveal my penis dressed for the role of Sloth in a medieval morality play, at the end of which it would no doubt be duly humbled by Prudence or Industry.

During this reverie Dr. Lay entered, stage left. After an exchange of pleasantries about the drive up from Mankato he said, "I'm beginning the circumcision now," which no one could mistake for a pleasantry.

—¤—

As the operation proceeded, Auntie sensed my need for distraction. She moved upstage and asked me about school. I explained that I was taking at least a year off, thinking of transferring somewhere out East. Then Dr. Lay, merrily snipping away, chimed in with, "Do you follow hockey much? I mean the Golden Gophers?"

No, I said. I didn't follow collegiate sports.

"Well, looks like they have a helluva team this year," he muttered, clearly dismayed at my failings as a conversationalist, as he went on snipping.

Later Dr. Lay dropped by the post-op room to give me orientation: an oral Owner's Manual, the do's and don'ts of your brand new penis. Most of the spiel concerned replacing the bandaging and fending off infection.

"Oh, one more thing," he turned to say, Columbo-like, before exiting my life forever. "For the next two or three weeks you're likely to experience intense discomfort when you have erections."

"Oh? What should I do about that?"

He shrugged. "Try not to have erections."

—¤—

It occurred to me some nights later as I stared up at the ceiling of my bedroom that I should have planned ahead: should have forced myself into a two-reps-a-day masturbation regimen just to get it all out of my system. But then I realized that I had been keeping to that very schedule anyway, more or less. I was still nineteen, after all.

At Pearlman's the next day, Lusty Lonnie Tyson from the Catalogue Department sashayed up to ask if I had any more of that good strawberry mescaline that we had shared a week earlier to celebrate her birthday. I was at first disheartened at my inability to meet her request, for surely that stash was long gone. And yet, as if by magic, I found a lump of foil in my jeans pocket that seemed to contain more than enough to light up both of our wretched factory lives.

"Let's go back to the stockroom," said the justly named Lusty Lonnie—and after all, it was I who had given her half of that name. We found a dark corner amid the boxes of stationery where we opened the foil and divided the pinkish powder into two equal mounds. I slurped mine down, then enjoyed watching Lonnie lap the foil clean with her sharp, tiny, cat-like tongue.

She turned her small Polynesian-hued face to me and smiled her shy, stunning smile as she thanked me and slowly tugged at the upper string of her halter top at the back of her wineglass stem of a neck, and just as I had always imagined, that one flimsy knot was all that held paradise at bay: the halter top slid down and Lonnie's life-sustaining organs wobbled free. They were pendular, mocha growths, like enormous twin teardrops designed to induce thousands more tiny teardrops of joy in their beholder, and instinctively my hands were rising to *ahhhhhhh-AHHHHHHHHHH!*

"*AAAAAAHHHHHHHHH!!!*" I screamed, pausing to add "*WOOOO-HAHHHHHHH!!!*" repeatedly until I had screamed myself and half the trailer park awake, and then kept on screaming while the camera panned farther and farther back a la the scene in the Hollywood producer's bedroom in *The Godfather*.

Wait—bad analogy. Any traces of blood in the bed? *Khartoum!*

No, we're clean.

My member still throbbed, though, still felt on the verge of exploding—and not in the *Penthouse Forum* sense of the word either, but rather in the President Kennedy's head sense. Lusty Lonnie, the stockroom, and finally

Pearlman Printing itself quickly dissolved. Normally, I would have tried to seize the fleeting vapors of a dream this splendid in order to sustain it as a semi-conscious fantasy until satisfaction had been achieved. But under the circumstances I had no choice but to banish Lusty Lonnie from my thoughts in favor of something repulsive. Grandma Naked just wasn't going to cut it this time. President Kennedy's head exploding—that was a good start…

Tommy Lasorda naked—*good*…

Freshly landed trout… *Yes…No, wait!* It's actually kinda sexy the way their mouths flap open and shut during their death throes…

Finding anti-erotic images to dwell on is tricky business when you're nineteen.

Haley knocked.

"Sorry, man," I said, "I just had one God-awful nightmare."

"Jesus," he moaned, wiping his eyes. "That's like, the third one this week."

I got rid of him quickly so that I could get to the bathroom. I needed to confirm that I hadn't actually burst the stitches this time. And if ever God, in one of Her puckish moods, had set out to design a penile stitch burster, Lusty Lonnie would have been the product. That girl was to penile stitches what Little Boy was to Hiroshima architecture, what Mad Dog Vachon was to the Very Capable Kenny Jay, what John Denver was to legitimate country rock: a Force of Nature, a Destroyer of Worlds.

There was a distressing, livid redness around the stitches but, thankfully, no bleeding. I began to question Dr. Lay's handiwork. He had cut too much; he had stitched too tightly; he had done this out of personal disdain. *If only I had boned up on college hockey*, I thought, and then immediately: *Not "boned up"; forget I said that!*

No, no. There would be no more boning up. *Try not to have erections* indeed… Easy for *that* ancient dried-up prune to say. He was forty if he was a day.

I went back to bed and imagined a hockey team of naked Lasordas staging a power play on a squad of dead, headless presidents: to sleep, perchance *not* to dream…

21. Meanwhile, Back at the Rat's[*]

The printing of a single wedding napkin—oh, what a thing of beauty it could be, were one suitably medicated for it. Here's how the pros went about it:

1) Load selected design into metal frame along with lead slugs bearing the names and dates; tighten.

2) Place frame into body of press.

3) Scurry to restroom; ingest drugs.

4) Fetch napkins of specified style and color from stockpiles; fan out on press's upper table.

5) While leaning against pelvis-level shelf, pluck virgin napkin from pile with right hand, slap onto feeding surface as press jaws part. Recoil as press automatically mashes napkin against foil and frame with a shuddering *thump*, leaving hot-stamped imprint.

6) When press jaws open, deposit finished napkin onto pelvis-level shelf.

---

[*] Note to punctuation purists: No, I can't justify that apostrophe; but the no-apostrophe version would feel even stranger, no?

7) Repeat…repeat…repeat…

Let's review Step 5—the one about the printer leaning against a pelvis-level shelf and the shuddering *thump*—while bearing in mind that the whole process was repeated up to thirty times a minute. In short, every two seconds the powerful impact of the press's jaws sent a small seismic wave through the wooden shelf and into the printer's pelvic bones, which generously passed those vibrations along to the nearest nerve clusters.

Normally this constituted an immense fringe benefit to the employee. Pearlman Printing in effect perfected the eight-hour erection decades before the first unsolicited Cialis advertisement ever wormed its way into a Hotmail account.

Given that I was still in the inital stage of my three-week rehabilitation from circumcision, however, mine was most definitely not a normal circumstance. Mine was a painful and trying circumstance, a time of long nights when sleep came only in twenty-minute snatches—*no don't say "snatches"!*—a time when a constant stream of stimulating vibrations to the pelvic nerve clusters for eight hours a day was not welcome in the least—and braless Denise Crawford working across the aisle with the side-cleavage popping out of her loose halter top wasn't helping either. Had these women no *shame*?

Even at home, my wounded little friend was always on my mind. When it flopped free from its bandage—so limp, so Lars Largo-like—it brought to mind images of the baby Jesus wrapped in swaddling clothes. I had no idea what swaddling clothes were, but it seemed like this gauze wrapped around the shaft in the shape of a hotdog bun might be the very stuff. I found myself involuntarily humming "Away in a Manger" during the long sit-down baths that Dr. Lay had insisted I take. The melody seemed to soothe it, to make the crisscross stitching glow less angrily.

While walking around in the course of a day, the bandaging gave me the illusion of great girth. Why, I could go out and butt-plug a Holstein if so inclined, I felt.

I was not so inclined; the very notion of butt-plugging a Holstein revolted me and normally would have been swiftly ejected from my thoughts; but under these very abnormal circumstances I seized upon the value of this random image like a prospector spying a gold speck in a dull gray pan of river gravel; I had been cataloguing just such images, and this new addition, that of having anal sex with livestock—wait, make that *constipated* livestock—soon found a niche somewhere between the Kennedy assassination and a bottomless, tirelessly jumping-jacking Tommy Lasorda in my mental pharmacopoeia of boner antidotes.

—▫—

I should not have been walking around in the first place, since walking creates groin-area friction. But suddenly the Missile had to be towed back to the garage yet again after some young rascals put popcorn in the gas tank.

"So was this shit popped or unpopped?" were Haley's first words.

"Was it popped popcorn or unpopped popcorn?" the police officer asked.

"We talkin' popped or unpopped popcorn here?" inquired the motorhead at Beautz Dodge, though it was hard to see how it mattered to him. I could only assume that he was yanking my chain for doubling off his associate at Wheeler Park several weeks earlier while out of my mind on THC.

So now I was doing an inordinate amount of walking, and doing it in an effeminate, mincing, tiptoeing manner so as to reduce intra-leg friction. My home run trotting days were over. But all such precautions were futile, of course. For even though I was no longer in college, I was still in a college *town* that was daily filling with college *women* as the fall semester approached.

College women haunted me at Pearlman's—in two shifts!—and were the bane of my existence. They and their damnably ubiquitous breasts, still prominently on display even as the days grew cooler. If Lusty Lonnie Tyson wasn't shining her high-beam headlights in my direction it was Trudi and her pert little points of order or Denise's huddled masses yearning to breathe free.

Not even all-male retreats like the James Court apartment offered much shelter, for women—especially their breasts—were forever being poetically waxed upon there. Even in those rare moments when breasts weren't the specified topic, they kept oozing into the banter metaphorically:

"Arnie brought a really *tits* new bong down from the Cities," Durward might say, and later Arnie might chip in with "*Muh*-gins, you missed the *tits*-est party last night in the apartment above the South Street." So deeply had the adjective* permeated the vernacular by 1975 that ironic usage had already become commonplace. "Oh, that's *tits*," Nielsen moaned when campus police kidnapped his Trans Am in lieu of payment for over fifty outstanding parking violations. "That's just *fuckin' tits*."

—¤—

After one trying day at Pearlman's processing orders, dodging mammaries, and defending my God-given flaccidity against all odds, I collapsed on my bed. No sooner had I drifted off to sleep than a fit of wild screaming roused me, which was predictable enough by that time, except that for once some other thoughtful souls had taken on the burden of vocalizing those screams on my behalf.

"*Tra-a-a-ai-le-e-e-er Mo-o-o-on-ste-r-rs! TRAI-LER MON-STERZ!!*" these voices implored, repeatedly.

The chant was accompanied by an alarming sensation of motion, as though the old home had decided of its own accord to reclaim its mobile status. The house began to pitch, the kitchen took a slitch; one probably gets the drift. And oh, what happened next was rich, at least to the cackling Meldom lads stationed outside beneath my louvered windows, mightily pleased with themselves for their invention of yet another puerile pastime, i.e. pounding on the bedroom walls of a trailer for thirty seconds and then fleeing, a.k.a. "Trailer Monstering."

"When do you get the Missile back?" asked Nielsen en route to the Rat's.

"Monday, they say."

"Now, was this popcorn popped or—"

"Unpopped."

"Nasty little fuckwipes. Oughtta take 'em out and shoot 'em," he opined

---

* "Extremely pleasing or successful; wonderful or superb; of high quality" *(American Heritage)*

while inducing his Trans Am to fishtail down Madison's slope for purely aesthetic reasons. Mental note: *Add "riding with Nielsen" to boner antidote stock.*

To Nielsen, there was no offense wickeder than an assault on a man's car. In his courtroom the insatiable cannibal Jeffrey Dahmer would have gotten off lightly ("Numb-nuts didn't even have the sense to throw out the leftovers," one could imagine him reasoning) compared to some gas-tank defiling infidel.

I minced my way through the Rat's front door badly in need of a drink. My odd gait drew relatively scant attention, though, compared to my order of a vodka sour. The customary options for first order at the Rat's ranged from tap to bottled beer. On a special occasion—say, a first Tuesday after a first Monday—shots of Jack could be added. But a vodka sour? The Rat's clientele raised a collective eyebrow while Nielsen articulated their collective concern.

"What the fuck you orderin' a girls' drink for?"

I might have explained to Nielsen that, due to my recent vanity circumcision, I now wished to consume beverages in smaller quantities so as to reduce trips to the Rat's privacy-free restroom, where a helpful neighboring urinator was almost certain to inquire as to whether or not I was aware that my member was wrapped up in a sanitary napkin and, within minutes, spread word of this eccentricity throughout the bar. And one could easily surmise the rest: by the end of the evening, everybody in the place is calling you "Tampon Dick," and within weeks complete strangers snigger and greet you as "T.D." the minute you set foot in the door, and before you know it you're in self-imposed exile from the Rat's and stuck with the Square Deal as your primary bar, where a biker chick takes a shine to you one night and her main man, "Tiny," follows you into the restroom for a few minutes of lighthearted banter, leading to eight weeks in traction. Ergo, I decided not to share.

"It's tasty," I assured Nielsen. "You want a sip?"

He glared at me as if I had just offered him one free week of trial access to my anus. I changed the subject to life in the new apartment, a topic to which he immediately warmed.

"Fuckin' Arnie—he's drivin' us fuckin' nuts," he said.

"Like how?"

"Okay, like I was vacuumin' the living room the other day," he said, triggering a mental image that was somehow harder to bring into focus than a naked, fungo-hitting Tommy Lasorda. "Arnie comes up, grabs the vacuum outta my hand and says, 'Nielsen, you're not *doin'* that right!' And then the little peckerwood tries to teach me how to *vacuum!*"

"He once castigated me for not falling out of an airplane the right way," I noted.

"See? See? Don't you get tired of that shit?"

"Actually, I think he might have saved my life."

"But it's like that *all the fuckin' time!* 'Yer not *cookin'* that right.' 'Yer not rinsin' the *glasses* right.' '*Yer not pourin' that right!*'" This last example was barked at the bartender who was mixing my second vodka sour in front of us. He flinched, understandably startled to find himself cast in the role of Arnie in the spontaneous reenactment of a domestic dispute, and it didn't help that he was already self-conscious about mixing vodka sours. At the Rat's, not even girls ordered girls' drinks.

The others started drifting in: Arnie, Cary, then Hoppy in turn silhouetted in the doorway by the blinding rays of the declining September sun, refugees from that heartless, raging inferno that is the world to this cool, dark oasis of reason. Twice more I would have to explain the absence of the Missile from the parking lot and field the inescapable popped-or-unpopped query. So went another night at the Rat's, the greatest bar on our glittering blue oblate spheroid.

We claimed a table in the ballroom even though there was no live music on weeknights, only Zeppelin classics blaring through the speakers, and then seized the stage to entertain the sparse crowd with our four-piece air-band routine. "The fuck is wrong with you, Muggins? You been walkin' like an old lady all night," noted Nielsen when I needed a hand to mount the stage.

But even the most basic of life's pleasures must be handled delicately when one's Best Boy is ringed in stitches. The pinball machine near the front door, with which I had bonded to the point where it seemed to grant me free games as soon as my familiar fingertips caressed its buttons, became a mortal foe. Those pelvic vibrations, again: trickier to steer clear of those than one might think. Besides,

Summer of Marv

nothing gave me harder erections than winning at pinball.

The new-fangled "Pong" thingamabob was a safer bet, so I lured Hoppy into a few rounds of it. This glowing, bleeping harbinger of the unfathomable Eighties stood out in the musty old bar like a white disco suit would have. Unlike disco, however, the video game was a wave of the future that we welcomed. If we could but master Pong, we would be well equipped to handle any innovations that the Gods of Technology might deign to chuck in our paths from here on out. Even jet backpacks. We were all hankering for those.

I was no more skilled at Pong than Hoppy was, and in fact had come to doubt very much that there was any such thing as Pong skill. My strategy consisted of reducing him to a giggling mound of blubber with japes and taunts—the same strategy I employed when Chest Boxing him—and it worked just as well.

As my Pong victory wound to a close, a stir arose behind us at the arrival of unexpected guests. I turned to see two prairie flowers of Meldom, one an MSU sophomore, the other just passing through. But the one just passing through, on her way back to school at St. Cloud, was the more familiar to me. It was Mary, Queen of Sots: Nielsen's ex.

It was Mary, yet it was not Mary. As I tiptoed toward the bar to greet her, she looked me straight in the eye and smiled. Gone were the long black bangs that had shielded her from an ungracious public. Gone was the shifty gaze. Gone, most conspicuously of all, was about thirty pounds of the old Mary, and that was a conservative guess. Thirty pounds was the approximate weight of Arnie's dog, which led, by transitive property, to the conclusion that Mary had lost more weight in sixteen months than could be crammed kicking and mewling into a medium-sized oven. A feat like that makes an impression.

This Mary was a far cry from the Mary of old. I wondered, as I embarked on a sightseeing tour of New and Improved Mary's attractions, if Nielsen had met her since dumping her more than a year previous. Of the thirty pounds that had gone AWOL, it seemed that every single milligram had been chipped from places that needed the chipping, as if a skilled sculptor had found the Venus lurking within a broad, slouching lump of clay.

"Mary," I said, cupping her hand in both of mine. "You're so... so..." Unable to come up with a euphemism, I just let it rip: "You're so *protuberant*."

"Thank you," she said with a smile that betrayed neither offense nor understanding.[*]

The New and Improved Mary, it turned out, had sprouted a personality. It was she who now took on the role of interrogator: *What are you gonna take this semester? Oh, you're not going back to school? Why not? So, what are you gonna do? Uh-huh. And how long do you figure to do that?*

It is a cliché to say that a woman has come to a bar dressed to kill, but Mary had come to the Rat's decked out in a manner that could have maimed had I let her form sink fully into my retinas. I had to treat her like an eclipse, looking straight into her for only a few seconds at a time, then turning away. In doing this I probably resembled her shier and lumpier incarnation of many moons past.

Inspiring as it was to chat with New and Improved Mary, I shuffled away as soon as decorum permitted. Even if I had been on the active roster that night I figured that I would not have had a chance with her, not with Nielsen around. He had been with Deb for nearly a year by then, it was true, but Nielsen had the great fortune to be born with both a conscience that went off duty at the third drink and reproductive equipment that didn't shut down until the tenth. "Was that a shoe?" I heard him saying somewhere behind me. *"Tell me that was a shoe!"*

I retreated for a while to the back bar—that Cone of Silence within the Rat's, where the Doobie Brothers reverberated faintly as if from another bar altogether—and, as was my duty under the Equal Time Provision of the Friendship Code, heard Arnie's version of keeping house with two Meldom lads. His countenance took on the usual "Oh what fools these mortals be" smirk of condescension that one had come to expect of him, but clearly Nielsen's hygienic habits had discomposed him. "He doesn't rinse the glasses thoroughly after he washes them," he whispered through trembling lips.

---

[*] "*Protuberant*—that was pretty good," Nielsen would tell me a week later. Meldom lads appreciate the *mot juste* when they hear it regardless of circumstance.

My duty thus fulfilled, I corralled Tom from Thailand, a figure I knew only from his cameo appearances at the Rat's and at after-bar parties, into a best-of-five Pong series. Unable to understand me any better than I did him, he was immune to my distracting witticisms; consequently, I proved to be no match for him. By the third trouncing, I began to suspect that his middle name might literally be Pong.

After a fifth vodka sour and the draining Pong marathon, I could postpone the inevitable no longer. I staked out the restroom until the coast was clear. Then, despite proceeding with unprecedented urgency, I had barely finished and tucked in before Durward sidled up next to me at the communal trough. It was a close call that signaled the need to call it a night. "Where's Nielsen?" I asked.

"Nielsen? He went home a while ago."

"With Mary?"

"Naw, no way. You believe what she did to herself? Wouldn't mind gettin' some of *that* lipstick on my dipstick."

Think distant thoughts—Lasorda thoughts. Dwell not on lipstick or dipsticks...

"Nielsen was supposed to give me a ride home!"

"You can walk it, can't you?"

"I'm way out of town, halfway to Eagle Lake!"

Durward continued to revel in his peeing and did not acknowledge my distress. It was typical of Durward to revel in such simple diversions: hot hoagies from Jake's Stadium Pizza, onomatopoetic replications of other people's sex acts, and long, leisurely urinations. He even reveled in his vomitings, or at least in post-hoc reenactments of them. He was a reveler of catholic tastes.

"This really sucks," I whined to a blurry collage of faces hovering over the bar. "Nielsen took off and now I don't have a ride home."

"*I'll* drive you home, Josh."

Somewhere the haunting showdown music from *The Good, the Bad, and the Ugly* echoed as I turned with a shiver to face Mary, Queen of Sots. The gentle, slightly askew smile on her face simultaneously conjured up the Mona Lisa and a lioness eyeing a limping gazelle, while several inches to the south her breasts continued to protuberate as obstinately as ever.

I was done for.

—¤—

A true woman of Meldom, Mary drove a pickup truck.

"So I hear that somebody actually put popcorn in your gas tank, eh?"

"Unpopped," I replied.

"Pardon?"

"Unpopped. The popcorn. It was unpopped popcorn."

"Oh."

"I just assumed you would want to know. So, it was unpopped. Just so you know."

"Uh-huh… And you're living in a trailer park now?"

"Yeah. Just go straight on 14. It'll be on the right. I'll tell you when we get close."

"You live there alone?"

"Doug Haley lives with me. Remember him?"

"Oh, yeah. Doug's a nice guy. You each got your own room?"

"Yeah. Doug's from Posterior Lake. Went back there for the weekend. That's how I ended up riding with Nielsen."

"So it's just you tonight."

"Ah."

I was learning how witnesses get duped into making hysterical confessions on courtroom dramas. There was a seductive lilt to her voice throughout our chitchat—not unlike the singsong tone of an unctuous district attorney. I was easily lulled into seduction, having built up no immunity to it. Getting picked up at a bar and driven home? By an achingly beautiful woman protuberating out of her embroidered blue work shirt? This just didn't happen to my ilk.

"Here's where you turn. It's the third one on the left after the speed bumps," I said.

Time was running out. I began to ponder how I might salvage something from this ill-fated rendezvous. What if—now here was a wild idea—what if I invited her in, got cozy with her to the extent that I dared, and then *just told her the truth?* And if she didn't believe me, I could unveil the proof. It occurred to me that she might have more to talk about with my penis than with me, seeing as both had shed a good share of their flesh recently. Then, if we hit it off, there might be dividends down the road the next time she happened to swing by Mankato. Or, for that matter, I might discover some pressing business that by chance would take me up to St. Cloud once my member and car were both back in working order! Sure! *That could work!*

But I was kidding myself; reality bit me in the form of a sharp twinge to my stitches as we jounced over the first speed bump. For one thing, there would be no getting cozy. The loosening of one more button on that work shirt was all it would take to blow me to smithereens. And anyway, at the end of the day—which we were quite literally approaching—I was merely a bit player in a revenge drama.

For, much as I would like to have believed that Mary simply wanted to acknowledge the courtesies that I had shown her during her dowdier days via a genial topless handjob or two, I knew that that was not the case. For Mary was insane, utterly barmy: *that* was the case. It had to be.

All those conjugal visits to Nielsen's dorm room…the four-hour bus rides from St. Cloud, only to be whisked to bed without so much as a shower…then forced to absorb every dram of conjugality that Nielsen could wring from himself in one night…all with Durward quite alert, notepad in hand, in the lower bunk… thence to be packed back onto a bus the following day…knowing Durward well enough to grasp that, upon her departure, the sounds of her and Nielsen's passion would be scrupulously reproduced before a packed studio audience…[*] God help her if she *hadn't* gone mad.

Now, having devoted every calorie of her energy to reforming herself, inside and out, into precisely the kind of woman that Nielsen would never think of dumping, the next step was to breeze through Mankato, make sure Nielsen got a good, long look at the goods he wouldn't be getting, and then— the final insult—give away those goods to his scrawny, dweebish best friend. A woman scorned, indeed. Revenge is a dish best eaten cold, the Mafiosi say; I was cannoli. As for dividends down the road, I was developing a sinking feeling that by the time my scars healed and I could make it up to St. Cloud,

---

[*] It suggested three meth addicts with plungers frantically unclogging an industrial toilet in a bid to retrieve a stash.

that prodigal thirty-pound Labrador would have returned to Mary's torso with an attendant regression in her self-esteem, a tragic *Flowers for Algernon*-like conclusion.

The truck jerked to a stop and Mary put it in park.

You have to do this just like jumping into a cold lake.

"You know, I could—"

"Gotta go, Mary. Thanks for the ride."

"Would you mind if I—"

"Great seeing you again. Let us know next time you're in town!"

And whatever she said next I did not hear over my own whining, as I minced briskly toward the safety of my corrugated metallic shell, where I soon cried myself to sleep.

22. Housewarming

"She didn't have any *arms!*" Arnie brayed, to a mixed chorus of *Whooaaaaa!*ing. "She just glared at me for a while, and then she dug into her bag and loaned me a pen with her *foot!*"

That was typical: All the cool stuff that made for great party chatter happened to Arnie. This seemed to be his sex substitute: dominating a room, commanding attention, mining anecdotal gold from his own faux pas, sucking *Whooaaaaa!*s out of inveterate *Whooaaaaa!*ers. I hated him at moments like this and evidently I wasn't alone. "To the ovens!" cried Durward, bearing Frances yet again toward the kitchen and certain doom.

The Armless-Lady-at-mass-registration anecdote premiered at a James Court party in late September, a housewarming affair held off until Arnie could render the apartment immaculate. And housewarming was an appropriate term on this unseasonably chilly night: guests arrived bundled in sweaters and coats. Just as I was regaining my physical tolerance for it, cleavage had scampered down its gopher hole into hibernation, not apt to be spotted again till May.

That was all right. Lusties and dudes alike were resplendent in their fall plumage. Not for the first time did I feel blessed to have been born into my generation, for surely mankind had reached the end of fashion evolution with our ascendancy. Thirty, fifty, a thousand years hence our center-hair-parting, Fu-Manchu-cultivating, shag-cut-sporting, curling-tong-wielding, light-blue-eye-shadow-applying, tattered-denim-wearing, Marshall-Tucker-Band-listening, huge-veiny-head-having progeny would look back in horror at the abominations that had preceded the Nineteen-Seventies and lionize us, for we had done to Bad Taste what Jonas Salk had done to polio. Then we'd see once and for all just who the Greatest Generation was.

Take the unknown female in a light blue peasant dress who had enjoyed Arnie's tale, for example. An elegant specimen of Seventies womanhood indeed. The dress was cinched at the ribcage with an elastic band, over which flowed pleasingly contoured globules of fatty tissue. Her auburn mini-fro and round glasses reminded one of the singer Phoebe Snow.

It was I who had greeted her upon her solo arrival and taken her denim jacket from her, which I had then laid carefully on Arnie's bed as per instructions. God forbid we should have guests' coats lying about in random places. For my money, if we were going to start being this fussy about entertaining, we might as well go whole hog and just declare ourselves a bridge club.

As her official greeter I had also given Peasant Dress the run-down on our selection of exotic beers and other fine beverages, and was fetching her a bottle of Miller while trying to figure out where I had seen her before. To unravel this mystery, I took the wholly unorthodox approach of asking her.

"We met at a party last winter," she said, downing half a bottle at one go as I eased her away from the unpleasant domestic spat brewing in the kitchen over the advisability of baking the dog with company present. "At Doug Haley's house?"

I shrugged. It didn't ring a bell.

"You and some other guys went outside and took off your shirts and started—I don't know… It was weird. You were like—like hitting each other…with your chests? You guys were pretty wasted."

I liked the way her smile slid to the right side of her face as she struggled to describe the scene, but I still couldn't place her. That could have been any of a dozen parties.

But it didn't matter. What mattered was that we were talking. And then a more remarkable thing occurred. Two adjacent seats opened up on the sofa. That in itself was merely fortunate; what made it remarkable was the fact that the seats had been vacated by Spook Blunt and a hominid with whom he had been engaged in a lengthy tête-à-tête—a hominid that bore markedly feminine characteristics. Not quite as markedly feminine as those of my new friend, but close.

"Let's have a seat," I said, somewhat dazed, as we swooped down to seize the Blunt-warmed sofa. En route, I found out that she had been called Nicky at that earlier party, and indeed still was. The unusual name provoked a mnemonic connection. The upcoming transfer to Mankato State of a Nicky had been a topic of lively discussion between Haley and his former housemate Barry, the notorious jewelry-store urinator, a Lurch-like, languorous fellow who had become uncharacteristically energized by the news.

"Ah, you're Barry's Nicky, then."

"'Barry's Nicky'?"

"Haley mentioned that Barry… He, uh… They, uh, knew someone from Posterior Lake who was transferring down here this year."

"Uh-huh. I'm sharing a house with some people on Fourth."

"Near Haley and Barry's old place?"

"No, it's way down by Madison."

"So you and Barry…"

We were interrupted by Barry himself.

"Hi, Nick. Bring any weed?"

"Sorry."

He shuffled away in dismay.

"So I hear you're that guy, huh?" asked Nicky.

I admitted that I was.

"Barry used to send some of your columns to me. You gonna write for the paper this fall?"

I explained to her that that was no longer an option, as I was not in school.

"Well, that's cool."

"Didn't know what I wanted to major in."

"Who does? That's why I transferred down. I couldn't figure shit out in the Cities. I figured it'd be mellower down here."

"Oh, definitely. It's a whole lot mellower compared with the Cities," said

I, who had spent a total of roughly twenty hours of my two-decade existence in the Cities. Most of those hours had been consumed watching Alice Cooper decapitate giant Muppets and having the crust of my penis sliced off. I could have brought these experiences to bear in order to buttress my argument re the singular mellowlessness of the Cities, but something told me it was wiser to maintain a Sphinx-like façade.

As we talked, she gradually leaned in toward me. A crease of cleavage snaked out over the top button of her dress and seemed to wink at me. There was just a hint of sway going on down there. *Is she not wearing a bra? They'd have to be uncommonly firm to hold up that way without a bra. More likely she's wearing a very loose one.* I allowed my gaze to venture downward, convinced to my private satisfaction that I was not perving per se, just trying to resolve an engineering issue.

"You're going to be around, though, right?" she asked, drawing me back to her face with no hint of incrimination. "I mean, even though you won't be in school."

There were unmistakable signs of her being interested in me. She was a good-looking woman who had arrived alone at a party, evidently not involved with Barry as I had hastily concluded, nor insane like Mary, and yet she seemed interested in me. There was a sudden impulse, wisely suppressed, to start unbuttoning her dress right then and there just to see if I woke up screaming once again in my bedroom at the trailer.

I yearned at that moment to tell her how much I adored the way her face hung off the end of her skull—the way the skin tucked in just so above her teeth and how it picked up her ears when she grinned. This really was a profoundly romantic sentiment as it took form inside my head, but in Mankato in 1975—or anywhere, anytime, I suppose—it was not a sentiment apt to lead to the spiritual-cum-carnal bonding that I craved. I could sense that.

Instead, because a mighty tag-team combo of mild inebriation and not so mild covetousness cooperated to whip cowardice into a turnbuckle, I heard myself say, "Maybe we could get together some time. Next weekend, say?"

While Nicky and I were negotiating the details of time and place, Nielsen and

Durward could be seen standing in their kitchen, grappling with a massive neurological short-circuit after observing Spook lead that same female-seeming entity by the hand into one of the bedrooms. Caribbean Indians watching Columbus's great ships approach on the horizon could not have appeared more shaken at the shifting of reality. The world as we had learned to navigate it was on the verge of extinction.

Regaining their senses quickly, for Meldom breeds resilient youths, they faced a dilemma. On one hand, the Gentleman's Code (Article IV, Clause 13, Sub-clause 25a) precluded knowingly making any intrusion into private space where one of us might be getting lucky. On the other hand, this was Spook.

They hit on a compromise: a proxy would have to be found. Just then, Barry sauntered up to make his inquiries re the whereabouts of weed.

Nielsen explained that some folks had just moments before ducked into the bedroom on the left to do a bowl of "some really tits stuff."

Barry was unmoved. "It's not that RoeWeed™ shit, is it?" he asked.

No, it was not, assured Durward, who could not resist adding that a Hefty bag of that very euphoriant could be had as a party favor just for the asking. Barry declined.

"Anyway," continued Nielsen, "they didn't want to share their shit with the whole party. But I bet they wouldn't mind one more joining in, 'cause I hear it's really mellow stuff."

"This room right here?"

"Yep."

Several seconds later, by which time I had joined them and received an update on current events, Barry returned, unstoned but edified. Though annoyed at being so crassly played, he was willing to be—in fact, insisted on being—debriefed.

"They were having some kind of sex," he said, "on top of all our coats." Sucking his teeth, he managed to add, "With all their clothes still on."

I said, "I know a guy who would claim that that doesn't count as sex."

23. Playing Time

"You have a nice touch, Josh."

"I do?"

"Oh, yeah."

"Should I just keep on doing this for the time being, then?"

"Oh, yeah."

It was my leisurely rotary-dialing of long-distance phone numbers that set off this exchange. I had gone through my parents' house, my aunt's number, and those of a few assorted high school friends back in Illinois. Fittingly enough, it was my dear departed grandmother's old number that finally closed the deal. It had two nines and a zero in it.

I *do* have a nice touch, I realized. I'm *not* totally unskilled. I have a technique! A style! *I have my own sexual idiom!*

It was the first time a woman had complimented me on any semblance of prowess, I noted to myself. Moreover, I further noted to myself that this was the first time I had ever been engaged in any sexual act of sufficient duration to be able to note things to myself while it was in progress.

Even a supportive lie on Nicky's part would have been welcome, but the preponderance of evidence suggested that she had indeed been enjoying my touch all over the place. And at that moment I was noting to myself *Girl, I could kiss you for saying something like that*, and then I realized that indeed, I could. After all, we were naked in bed together. Kissing ought to be in play.

So I kissed her. And kissed her again. And all the while I kept on doing

Summer of Marv

the thing that I had been doing that made her say *Oh, yeah*, and it soon became clear that we were playing extra innings tonight.

This is great! Good old fingers with their built-in, never-let-you-down skeletal structure, I noted, now noting my ass off. *This is working! It's really working! It's like thousands of tiny fingertips urging-- Hey! Look at that! Look at what's happening! Wow!... Wow...*

After a breather, Nicky reciprocated the nice-touch favor and then sprang a nifty twist ending on me more satisfying than anything ever seen at the end of a *Barnaby Jones* episode. The renovated equipment was working just fine. Nothing exploded except what was supposed to explode. *This is better than sex,* I mused as the world grew pleasantly dark. *This is—well, I would dare coin a phrase and call it "making love"! This is...*

The resolution of this chain of thought would have to wait. There would be no more thoughts for a while, no more noting things—no, not until, somewhere in the foggy mists of a very pretty, far-off land, I heard Nicky sigh:

"Awwww, *shiiiit!!*"

...at which moment the covers flew off the bed—Nicky's bed—which was bouncing, *Exorcist*-style.

Then Nicky was out of bed, naked and aglow, painted in stripes by the morning light seeping through the slats of her Venetian blinds, her unbound boobs heaving Hither and Yon and then back to Hither again before making another mad rush for Yon before she captured the rampaging blobs in a beige bra. For all that aerobic activity they didn't appear to be sweating, but it was hard to tell, and she was too busy rooting through dresser drawers and tossing garments onto the bed to be bothered with the question.

"I'm really sorry, Josh. I overslept! I gotta be at work in twenty minutes!" As she explained this, she stood facing me at the foot of the bed, legs shoulder-length apart, still bottomless, vigorously rubbing deodorant into her unshaved armpits.

No apologies were necessary. If it had not already been in my mind to send Nicky a very cordial thank-you note for the prior evening's hospitality, the deal was sealed at that moment.

"Go back to sleep! Help yourself to anything in the kitchen! Talk to you later!" She kissed me and then ran out the door. *I must remember to note her address as I'm leaving,* I decided. *It would be nice to find out her surname, too.*

—¤—

I had the whole day off and could have spent a relaxing morning sniffing all her bras, laundered and dirty alike—but at that point, it seemed redundant. Even *wrong*, somehow.

I got dressed and walked out into a crisp, cool, early October morning. I set the Missile's coordinates for Front Street, then Spring Street, then past the Haley Ruins on Fifth, each sight spurring its own memories of my year as a flaming, unabashed, out-of-the-closet Minnesotan.

There was Michael's, the restaurant where Jan Kelso had conducted her mini-seminar on how to take a lady out, the lessons of which I had finally made good use with Nicky the night before. And now here was the Rat's, where Nicky and I had danced later on at my suggestion—a notion that would never have popped into my head had I not been schooled by Ingrid's friends in the significance that the ritual held for females. Perhaps I was not entirely uneducable after all.

The winter and spring had been a series of short, stressful outbreaks of loveless sex; the summer a long, slow taffy-pull of sexless love. One of these days, I was going to have to corral these two squirrelly kids, Love and Sex, into the same room and make sure we all got acquainted. One of these days perhaps very soon.

—¤—

That very afternoon I rounded off the nostalgic tour by visiting McElroy, more specifically the F-wing room of Spook Blunt. My purpose was not to pick his brain on the whole sex-love dichotomy, for to do so would have been roughly as fruitful as asking Nielsen for housekeeping tips, but merely to pay a social call. We had not met since the James Court party a week before, and he had phoned repeatedly to invite me since then.

His woolly, whitish hair still rose off his head like an interstate on-ramp, but he had grown it out more over the summer. Combined with the way his head flowed necklessly into his body, the steep diagonal slope of his coif suggested a sort of less flexible, sedentary Gumby.

He was now the lone survivor among us in the dorm, holding out there into his third year at school, the last Mohican. He had obviously made a home for himself; I found him, cigarette in hand, ensconced in the room's lone chair, thus compelling me to sit on his unmade bed.

"So how's it going with that fine chick you met at the party?" he asked.

I told him we had had a pleasant date and that we would be going out again on the weekend. A pregnant silence followed, during which it was hard to avoid pursuing the same chicks-met-at-last-week's-party theme. I told him I had witnessed the unchivalrous interruption he had been forced to endure in the bedroom at James Court. What, I asked, had happened after that?

He took a long, thoughtful draw on his Marlboro and heaved four tufts of smoke upward through crisply puckered lips, as if trying to alert the rest of his tribe as to the exact location of the cavalry, and then said with a terse shrug (the only genre of shrug he could manage), "Brought her up here and smoked some pot and, well, you know…fucked her."

To look at him, one would think this sequence of events no more extraordinary to him than ordering a poor boy from Kato Pizza and awkwardly overtipping the delivery boy. I expressed skepticism in the most vehement terms.

"I'm telling you, I *fucked* her, man! Right *there!* On that bed you're sitting on!"

"Spook, you're creeping me out."

"Check it out. Just check it out! Right *there!*"

"What? Where?"

"Where your hand is. Don't you *see* it?"

I looked down to the area on Spook's bed sheet where my left hand rested. Now it was my turn to become the uncomprehending noble savage watching the impossibly large ships loom in. I suspect a vague, uneasy blankness swept across my face, soon displaced by bug-eyed, teeth-baring horror.

My hand lay in the epicenter of a large eggshell-white stain. It was dry. It was crusty. It was enormous. A frisky young dictator whose career was just that year shifting into high gear over in a prominent Middle Eastern country, had he been flown in to inspect the site, would have promptly proclaimed it the Mother of All Semen Stains. It went on and on, spanning time zones of bed-sheet surface. It had mountain ranges, steppes, deserts, frosty tundra, hidden oil reserves, peninsulas; several archipelagos lay within its vast territorial waters.

"You know what that *is*, don't you?" he asked, giving me a cold, penetrating, homeroom-teacher stare over the wire rims of his glasses.

The scales fell from my eyes and were quickly swallowed up by the scaly monstrosity into which they plunged. I now recalled the phone call I had received from him the very day after the party—the sudden, urgent need for me to come up to his room and, *you know, just listen to some records and get wasted, man*. Then the persistent follow-up calls when I had not shown.

"Well, what does *that* prove?" I stammered. "You could have done that on your own."

At this he became agitated. Had he possessed a neck, its hackles would have been raised. "I'm telling you, I *fucked* her, and then she didn't have any birth control, see? So I pulled out at the last minute"—one had to admire the cagey way Spook implied the passage of plural *minutes*—"and just shot it all over the bed. Right there."

"Good God, man. That was a week ago."

"Well, I thought it would be rude to shoot *on* her, you know," he continued, "'cause we just met." Dumbfounded, I was forced to imagine his companion diving for cover as Spook's enraged gonads sprayed forth twenty-two years of pent-up frustration.

I mulled offering him all the quarters in my possession and reminding him that the basement laundry room was open all hours, but I did not want to rile him further. A man with reproductive organs capable of all that… Well, what if he should decide to turn them on *me?* A few quick strokes and I might be pinned to the wall like a fly in a spider web. Do-gooders had been admitted to the Legion of Super Heroes with less prodigious powers than this.[*]

"Um…congratulations, Spook."

---

[*] I wasn't staring at you, Bouncing Boy, I swear. But hey, if the shoe fits…

Summer of Marv

"No big deal, man," he said, snuffing out his Marlboro and reaching into a drawer for his stash of primo RoeWeed™.

Well, what the heck. I could no longer deny that Spook had achieved intercourse. I still had my doubts about that enormous stain, though, and for a moment I suspected him of bribing some large-animal vet for several syringes of leftover horse semen, only to conclude that Spook would never have shown that much initiative.

Patience—now, that was his strong suit. He was certainly capable of preserving the crime scene as long as necessary until a corroborating witness could be lured to it. Surely some of the outlying provinces had been added at a later date, but the heartland of the stain was authentic. And with the yielding of my tacit confirmation, somewhere the Great Scorer was unfurling his Finger of Fire to carve Stanley "Spook" Blunt's name into the roll of nonvirgins. It was something that could never be taken away from him, not unlike achieving full tenure in the Faculty of Manhood.

After a thorough scouring of my hands, I settled in and, acquiescing to Spook's plan, got loaded with him, and we two sexually active Caucasoid-Minnesotan studs "got down" and "rapped" about "Chicks, man. Chicks. I mean, who knows what weird shit goes on inside their heads, right? Can't live with 'em; can't live without 'em."

24. Beer Run

Marijuana Mike and his housemates held a kegger at stately Marijuana Mike Manor on Parson Street early in Fall Quarter. The keg ran low near sundown; Nielsen and I volunteered for the run.

I had hoped to see Nicky at the party but she had not appeared. Things with Nicky were not progressing as quickly as I had hoped; like everything else in the Ford Administration, our relationship seemed headed for stagflation.

Still, my stats were moving in the right direction even as I was feeling less and less need to keep track of them. So Sex might take care of itself, and as for Love? As that ascetic philosopher Karen Carpenter kept telling us via AM radio, Love may grow, for all we know…

We heard that oldie wheezing from the Missile's radio as Nielsen and I tried to reach a consensus on which liquor store to patronize. He was unusually disputatious during those early autumn days due to his own relationship turmoil. There had been tension between Deb and Val of late, which concerned him re possible spillover effects on his friendship with Haley. He had even come out to the trailer the evening before to smooth things over, but Haley and Val had gone out.

"You can't even take these stupid concubines out to a bar together anymore," he had grumbled in my kitchen. "They spend the whole night hissin' and barin' their claws at each other… It's fuckin' sickening."

"If we're not careful, chicks will wreck our whole group," I said, sounding oddly Spook-like in my sudden expertise on chick psychology. "We could end up just like the Beatles."

"No, we *won't* end up like the Beatles," Nielsen spat back. "Goddam cum-bucket British turdbinders, anyway…"

"Well, then. Wanna go to the mall and fondle manikin tits?"

"Hell, yeah!"

Later, I led him on a quick round of Trailer Monstering down the street from my unit. Now that I could run again I had taken up the sport myself. Trailer Monstering was becoming the new Chest Boxing.

On our beer run we took our time, sharing a pipe while we cruised along to spur the as yet unfelt effects of chocolate mesc.

"Well, sweat glands is what they *are*," Nielsen said, "Aren't they? I read that somewhere."

"Yeah, but what does that mean? Do they themselves actually sweat? Or do they just *make* the sweat to send out to other body parts?"

"Got me. Hey, swing down Front Street here, why doncha?"

Just as I made the turn, the latest John Denver hit came on and the mesc throttled both of us simultaneously.

"Turn that shit up!" Nielsen commanded, though by then my arm was already speeding toward the volume knob. We rolled down our windows to let the chilly October air tickle our faces and let "Calypso" soar out to the world. Past the Gurdy and the South Street we cruised, and near the Club Royal, no longer able to hold back, we began to sing along:

Aye, Calypso! We somethin'-somethin' spirit!
Somethin'-somethin'-somethin', somethin' and so well
Hi-de-heyyyy-diiii
Di-di-di-di-di-di…

It would have made for a nicer memory if bar-crawling pedestrians all along Front Street had stopped in place and joined with us on the screeching falsetto chorus, as tends to happen in romantic comedies of late-Nineties vintage. In real life they did not so oblige us, of course, but merely stopped and stared.

We did not mind. This was our Eureka moment: we had finally hit upon just the right cocktail of drugs and alcohol to attune us—now, near the end of a year in which the singer had inflicted "Sweet Surrender," "Thank God I'm a Country Boy" and "I'm Sorry" in rapid succession upon an unsuspecting radio-listening public—to the creative wavelength of John Denver. Now we knew how Edison had felt when he decided to trot out the ol' carbon filament just to give it a whirl. As we warbled along to the "Calypso" chorus, our bodies metronoming left and right, we suddenly realized that John Denver was a bona fide bowl-cut-sporting genius and that this was *the greatest song that any human had ever recorded in history!*

Ho-dee-hoooo, yeeeeee
Di-di-di-di-DEEEEE...

Mettler's and then the Rat's hove into view as the chorus see-sawed on and on, and it was still 1975 out there in the purple twilight, where divorce and detox and depression and home-detention sentences and all the other indignities that the unpaid fiddler would later heap upon us could yet be deferred, perhaps forever. For that one shimmering moment, even Nielsen had made his peace with John Denver, the lion lying down with the lamb, and God saw that it was good.

—¤—

The following Monday I was excused from the afternoon shift at Pearlman's two hours early on account of feeling well. This condition was a function of the same mescaline that had had such a salubrious effect on Nielsen and me, the source of which had been Pam, a tall, stoop-shouldered napkin newbie at Pearlman's who had quickly proved herself an invaluable source of mescaline, dummy dust, and windowpane. She even offered free samples to ensnare our souls, like the dealers on the juicier *Dragnet* episodes did. Just a crackerjack dealer all around, a real find.

I had been on one of my drug-free health kicks since Marijuana Mike's party had ended some thirty-two hours earlier but finally succumbed to temptation when the departmental message board was edited during lunch to read:

Smile! It's
MARV'S
birthday today!

Well, I reasoned, if freeborn Americans couldn't celebrate their supervisor's birthday with a jot of watered-down acid blotted in Nestlé's Quik, then for what had all those brave men given their lives in the Revolution? I bought a whole round of the stuff, lit myself up, gave Cary and Hoppy each a pinch, and took some over to Lusty Lonnie, who was delighted, though not enough so to untie her halter top, which was a shame now that I stood a fair chance of surviving the sight.

My work was still only half done, I knew, so I told Marv that my stomach felt funny, which was true enough: at that moment I found my stomach unbearably hilarious, the Richard Pryor of vital organs. I received the great man's blessing to leave, which was lucky, since I could not have resisted the temptation to curl his noble Roman hair in my fingers much longer.

I picked up a mescaline doggy bag and stepped out into the bracing air of a clear autumn afternoon. I had no place to get to, no homework to do, no books to write, no taxes to file, no foreskin to clean out, no responsibilities at all beyond keeping the Missile's gas tank popcorn free. I headed for James Court, where lesser temptations than free mesc could lure the lads away from their studies. A new episode of *The Bionic Woman* had been known to suffice.

Before long we all had Millers in our hands and the vile residue of RoeWeed™ in our lungs as we stood on the patio watching Frances make impossible leaping grabs of the Frisbee, and then somebody said "This is the last Miller," and somebody else said "I bought the last case," and then Arnie admitted that it was his turn to buy, and I volunteered to drive.

—⌑—

"Oh, aren't the trees *pretty!*" Arnie cooed as we crunched our way across the lawn over the season's first layer of fallen leaves, for so glorious was the color scheme erupting all around us that not even Arnie could recommend refinements.

It would be over soon, of course. Minnesotans—poseur Minnesotans included—possess this curious, perennially self-renewing capacity to believe that they can actually enjoy a fully-formed autumn of crisp, cobalt-sky days like this one, only to wake up one morning in early November and find the trees more thoroughly denuded than Donna James at Last Call and a cruel sheen of frost on the ground.

Autumn in Minnesota is all the more glorious for the brevity of its motley reign. And in its way, as I look back now from this cozy twenty-first century perch, it was not unlike the Seventies: crowded out on the one side by the relentless, mosquito-plagued summer of the Sixties and then, before it could dig in its heels, knocked flat by a merciless, bullying wind of Reaganomics, hair metal, glossy-chested action heroes, and, of course, AIDS that was even then rolling relentlessly down from the Arctic to sap the color from our mesc-warmed cheeks.

In the Missile, Arnie and I made the steep climb up Stadium Road toward campus with the sun at our backs and a painfully deep blue cloudless sky swaddling us. Our goal was the liquor store off the far side of campus near Nielsen's old Broadmoor apartment.

"*Muh*-gins, this is the *tits*-est mesc," he purred. "Get more if you can."

Later I would recall that day when I considered all he had gone through. For of all those in my immediate circle Arnie appeared the least likely candidate to be drafted and sent to the front lines when The Big One for our generation would break out not so many years later. And yet serve and fight he did, and with distinction, logging untold hours in hospital wards, doing whatever he could to make the slow, messy crossing-over of friend after friend just a little less terrifying. Miraculously uninfected himself, the persnickety lad who valued nothing so much as order and neatness and having things just so would learn to cope with chaos and decay while helplessly watching loved ones wither away like the leaves that crumbled under our shoes in the liquor store parking lot.

Still nineteen and still immortal on this October afternoon, we breezed past Ellis on Stadium Road and felt the earth drop out from under us. Hitting that hill on mesc was like diving out of the Cessna again. At that moment, the woods beyond Stoltzman Road unfurled before us on the horizon: a perfect Trix cereal bowl of reds, yellows and oranges with stubborn splashes of deep coniferous green here and there, all awash in the slanting rays of the declining sun. It looked as if God, in a jealous hissy fit, were saying, "*Here's* how it's done, Monet. Unfuck *you*." Then, as if sent to underscore that point, a gentle breeze rippled slowly across the enormous canvas left to right, bidding every tree to genuflect and every molecule in our spinal cords to burst into cold flame.

I lifted my foot from the Missile's accelerator. Gravity would pull us home now. We coasted onward in silent awe of God's wonders, both natural and pharmaceutical. Behind us lay a case of cold beer and in front of us a tableau of stupefying beauty. In between were friends who would be glad to see us, perhaps even after discovering that we had bought Hauenstein.

"Muggins, if we died right now," Arnie whispered, "it would be all right," to which I offered not a word of dissent.

Index

Personally, I have a soft spot for meandering tales packed with loads of odd, sketchy characters who shine briefly only to disappear without warning. Such narratives aptly portray real life as most of us live it, not to mention the Democratic presidential primary process.

I assume that you don't hate such stories either if you have made it this far, although most likely you prefer the books of this sort written by writers with actual talent—your Tolstoys, your Dickenses, your Anthony Powells. Well, say what you will about my style, I've got one thing that those dead white mofos haven't got—an Index! No need here to flip through back pages muttering darkly, *Thurman Lee... Black guy on the dorm floor or Pip's benefactor?* It's all right here in alphabetical order, at no extra charge and with no claims whatsoever to accuracy.

academic probation, 49
Achievable Girl, 101-02
acid, (see *LSD*)
Adam magazine, 27
Airplane Spin, 66
Al, 67-68
Albert Lea, Minnesota, 116
Algonquin Round Table, 70
Allman Brothers, 56
American Graffiti, 113, 114
American Revolution (as justification for workplace drug abuse) 151
American Wrestling Association (AWA) 6, 65-66, 73, 101
amphetamines, 3, 14, 37, 95, 108, 135; as softball performance enhancer, 98, 99-100
Anderson, Wendell, 7
Angela, 27, 31
Antietam, 21
Arboleda family, 69, 73, 84-85
Arboleda Prodigal Son, 86, 91
Arboleda, Laura, 65-66, 69, 70, 71, 85-86, 90-91, 95, 112-15, 117
Arboleda, Mr., 66, 70, 73, 82 ; compromised brain of, 85, 86
Arboleda, Mrs., 66, 69-70, 85, 113
Arboleda, Rosa, 65-66, 69, 70, 71-73, 81-83, 85-87, 90-91, 95, 112-15, 117; aggressive shotgun-calling of, 112; wrestling prowess of, 66, 86, 87
Armless Lady, 137
Arnie, 2, 3-4, 23-27, 30, 33, 47, 61-64, 84-85, 95, 104, 105, 118-20, 128, 131, 132, 137-38, 151-53; enviable circumcised state of, 105; incidental

gayness of, 26-27; Napoleonic qualities of, 120, 130; public urination charge and, 59; uncanny global warming foresight of, 23; *Unfuck you* curse coinage and, 50
AWA (see *American Wrestling Association*)
"Away in a Manger" 126
Aztec deities, 73
Bardolf, 75, 77
Barnaby Jones, 143
Barry, 37, 59, 139-41
Batcave, the, 59
Batman, 13
Beatles, the, 47, 106, 149
Beautz Dodge, 99, 127
Belgrade Avenue Bridge, 19
Berra, Yogi, 101
Betty Jo and Trevor, 42
binge drinking, 37
Bionic Woman, The 151
black holes (as weak, overused metaphor), 12, 69, 113-14
Blizzards of the Century, 1
Blunt, Stan (Spook), 37-38, 43-46, 95, 139, 141, 144-47, 149; Acid Incident and, 46; congenital necklessness of, 43, 44, 145; ferocious gonads of, 146; flagrant virginity of, 45 (see also *Mother of All Semen Stains*)
Bobick, Duane, 6, 7
Bockwinkle, Nick, 6, 65-66
Bodega, the 36
bongs, 3, 19, 119, 128
Bonnie, 14, 32
Bouncing Boy, 146
Bowie, David, 89, 90, 103 (see also *Young*

Americans)
Bozo, 57
Brady Bunch, The, 45
Brady, Marcia, 45
Brannigan's, 116
bra-sniffing, 92, 98-99, 103, 104, 144
bralessness, 57, 58, 126
bras, 31, 105, 140, 143 (see also *bralessness, bra-sniffing*)
breasts, 61, 127-28, 133; of mall minikins, 149 (see also *tits*)
Broadmoor Apartments, 1, 4, 152
Brunzell, Jim, 65 (see also *High Flyers*)
Burton Hotel, the, 69, 115; lobby mummies of, 69, 116
butterbrown potatoes (Yum Yum Inn delicacy), 35, 36
Caledonia, the 36
"Calypso", 149-50
campus police, 128
Cap'n Dave, 24-25
Carpenter, Karen, 148
Cary, 39-41, 69, 75-77, 89-91, 95 98-99, 116, 130, 151; belligerent dance stylings of, 98, 101-02; Clintonesque sex-defining by, 121; as mastermind of anti-Marv conspiracy, 95, 97; pick-up technique of, 101-03
Casablanca, 21, 59
Cash, Johnny, 35-36
Chad, 41, 74, 116
Chaney, Lon, 116
chaos theory, 61
Charge of the Sperm Brigade, 22
Chef, the, (see *Happy Chef*)
Cheryl, 68, 87, 111
Chesney Auto Parts, 99, 107-09
Chesney Methedrine Massacre (see *Chesney Auto Parts*)
Chest Boxing, 12, 21, 49, 131; superseded by Trailer Monstering, 149
Christ, Jesus, (see *God, the Lord Our*)
Chucky, 87
Cialis, 126
Cindi, 24, 26, 31
Circe, 71
Cities, the, 84, 90-91, 128, 139-40; as source of quality drugs, 62; as source of racist faculty, 44, 46; as site of elective surgery, 121-22
City Mouse, 33, 60
Cocker, Joe, 72
"Cold Ethyl," 91
Columbo, Lieutenant, 122
Columbus, Christopher, 141
concubines, 33, 34, 72, 102, 105, 114, 148
Cooper, Alice, 90-91, 111, 140
Cooper, James Fenimore, 80

cops (see Mankato Police Department)
crank (see *amphetamines*)
Crawford, Denise (braless napkin printer), 126, 127
Crusher, The, 6
crystal, (see *amphetamines*)
Dachau, 4
Dad (of JM), 7, 112
Dahmer, Jeffrey, 129
Dante (Alighieri), 117
Dating Game, The, 67
Davidson, John (chronically disappointing *Tonight Show* guest host), 48
Dax grease (condescendingly used as symbol of the Fifties), 113
Deb, 92, 103, 132, 148; self-hosted birthday party of 103-04; culture-spanning sluttiness of, 92
Democrats, perceived treachery of, 53
dental hygienists, 48-49, 71, 75, 88
Denver, John, 53-54, 97, 124; Nielsen and JM's latent admiration for, 149-50
Derringer, Rick, 30
Devonshire (apartment complex), 33
Diamonds, the, 113
Dobermans, 117
Dodge Challenger, 17, 18, 80 (see also *Missile, the*)
Don't Cry Now, 90
Doobie Brothers, the, 132
dorks, carload of, 26
dorm kegger, 13, 49
Double Vertical Forward Suplex, 71
drug and alcohol abuse, 1-153 *passim*
Dude magazine, 27
dummy dust, 150
Durward, 2, 3, 4, 14, 32, 33, 40, 47, 59, 79, 80-81, 95, 105-06, 110, 128, 133, 135; as bête noire of Spook Blunt, 44-45, 141; as Chest Boxing pioneer, 12; as *Ur*-Trailer Monster, 128; as victim of Marnie-induced psychic trauma, 106; Baron von Raschke obsession of, 66; dog-baking and, 120, 137; Flintstonian characteristics of, 45; marijuana farming and, 81, 119 (see also *RoeWeed*™); mimicking other people's sex acts and, 135; poetry of, 32, 60, 105; Tarzan-like ululations of attack of, 12; vomiting and, 81, 133
Dylan, Bob 6, 88-89, 111
Eagle Lake, Minnesota, 133
Eagles, the, 72, 90, 113
Electric Light Orchestra, 113
Ellis Avenue, 153
Exorcist, The, 106, 143
Faculty of Manhood, 147
Fantasy Hit Parade, 71
Fast Eddie, 99
Fendrich, Wolfgang, 47-48, 49

Fiat convertible, 92
Field House, 47
Fight Club (as anachronistic analogue for secrecy enshrouding dental hygiene clinic), 49
Figure-four Leg-lock, 86
fire marshal, 68, 70-71, 94
fire-alarm pulling, 41
Firpo, Pampero, 7
First Amendment absolutism (as applied to massage parlors), 28
flesh-eating virus, 87
Flopalong Cassidy, 27-29, 31
Flowers for Algernon, 136
Ford, Gerald R., 51, 54-56, 57, 85, 148
Ford Galaxy, 90
Ford Torino, 7
foreskin, 104, 151; trimming of, 121-22
Frances, 119-20, 137, 151
Franklin, Aretha, 111
frat boys, 20, 21, 25, 58, 74; odiousness of, 43, 48
Freddie, 24-27, 41; and Jack Nicholson, 34
Free Press (see *Mankato Free Press*)
French salon society, 97
Friendship Code, 132
Front Street, 27, 28, 32, 58-59, 64, 144, 149
Fu Manchu moustaches, 38, 53, 67, 137
Funky Chinamen (from Funky Chinatown), 72
Gagne, Greg, 65-66, 82
Gagne, Vern, 6, 65
Garrett, Leif, 80
Gay Nineties, the (bar), 91
Gent magazine, 27
Gentleman's Code, 141
Glenwood Avenue, 26
GMC pickup truck, 105
God, the Lord Our, 18, 45, 53, 58, 112, 114, 124, 128, 135, 147; name of spoken in vain, 23, 26, 84, 96, 118, 138, 146, 149, 150, 153; gratuitous mishief-making in JM's sex life by, 28, 124 (see also *"Thank God I'm a Country Boy"*)
Godfather, The, 123
Golden Gophers ice hockey team, 122
Good, the Bad and the Ugly, The, 133
Graduate, The, 3
Graham, Moonlight, 15
Graham, Superstar Billy, 66
Grandma (of JM), 92-93, 142; serviceable nakedness of, 93, 124
Grant, Bud, 5
Grant, Ulysses S., 6, 17
Greco-Roman Knuckle Lock, 66
Gronky, Helen, (see *Helen of Waterville*)
Gumby, 145
Gurdy (see *Hurdy Gurdy*)
Haley, Doug, 10-12, 14, 15, 37, 38, 51, 52, 59, 92, 112, 119, 124, 127, 134, 138, 139, 144; evil landlord of, 11, 52; house on North Fifth of, 11-12, 37, 138, 144, 148; improbable culinary skills of, 37, 119
Half Nelson, 82
half-loaded caulking gun, 111
handjobs, 22, 30-31, 67-68, 121, 135; underratedness of, 30
Happy Chef (diner), 10, 36, 106
Happy Chef (pagan spoon-wielding totem), 10, 14, 106, 112, 144
Harry's Hofbrau Haus (the Delmonico's of pre-disco Katoland), 69, 104, 116
hat shitter, 38, 108
Hate Red Day, 107-09
Hauenstein beer, 1, 5, 153
Health and Hygiene course, 48, 49
Hedley G. (see *Stonebridge, Hedley G.*)
Heenan, Bobby, 117
Heimlich maneuver, 29
Helen of Waterville, 104, 105
Hennig, Larry "The Ax", 66
Henry IV, 74
Herman (Motorhead Laureate of Meldom), 80
Heterosexual League, 16, 34
"Hey Jude," 47
High Flyers, the, 65, 86, 117
Hiniker Cab, 99
hippies, 14, 51, 59
Hiroshima, 124
Hitler, Adolf, 4
Ho Chi Minh trail, 54
Hoffman, Dustin, 3
Holmes, Sherlock, 80
Holsteins, 126
Hoover, Herbert, 6
Hoppy, 69, 75-76, 78, 116, 130, 131, 151; alleged attainment of second base with Helen of Waterville by, 104; appalling effects of amphetamines on, 100, 108
Hotmail, 126
Hurdy Gurdy, the (frat-boy haunt), 26, 58-59, 149; lecherous-as-monkeys bartenders of, 92
Hutts (as anachronistic analogue for sheet-metal workers' wives), 107
"I'm Not in Love," 72, 84, 91
"I'm Sorry," 150
Illinois, 6, 7, 8, 92, 121, 142
impotence, 28
Industrial League, the, 74, 97, 99, 108
Ingalls, Pa, 119
Ingrid, 10, 13-15, 16, 18, 22, 32-33, 49-50, 102, 144
Ingrid's vagina, 9-10, 12, 13, 21, 33, 49, 50, 55, 93; as metaphor for all things terrifying, 59
intercourse, (see *Ingrid's vagina*) (see also *handjobs, Holsteins*)

156

Introduction to Poetry, 46
Iranian students, 48
Iron Sheik, the, 117
Jack and Larry, 69-70, 71, 94, 115
Jackson, Andrew, 55
Jake's Stadium Pizza, 133
James, Donna, 58, 60-63, 152; as feminist icon, 58
James Court apartments, 104-05, 118-20, 127, 151; housewarming party and, 137-41, 144-45
James Gang Rides Again, The, 12
Janesville, 26
Jay, the Very Capable Kenny, 6-7, 124; as metaphor for JM's sexual ineptitude, 50; as analogue for impotence of Ford administration, 55
Jennings, Waylon, 116
jet backpacks, 131
Jews, 3
Jimbo, 4-5
Jimmy, (Yum Yum Inn proprietor) 35-37
Joan, 14, 32-33
John, Elton, 90
Johnson, Lyndon, 56, 57
johnson (JM's), 30-31, 104, 121-24, 134-35, 140; likened to baby Jesus, 126
Judd, 60
Juggs magazine, 11
Julius II (impatient Pope), 69
Justice League of America, the, 13
Karras, Father Damien, 106
Kato Ballroom, the, 113-14
Kato Engineering, 99
Kato Pizza, 145
Kelso, Jan, 18-20, 21, 22, 55, 71, 144; nasal-hair bewitching perfume of, 19; nonexcreting properties of, 18
Kennedy, John F., 56; exploding head of, 123, 124, 127
Kent, Roger, 101
Kevin, 86-87, 112-14, 117
KEYC, 53
Khartoum, 123
Kortig, Lenny, 74-75, 77
KTOE, 1, 149
Lam, 87-89, 93-94, 115; as victim of domestic violence, 110-111; incompetent Dylan-appreciating by, 88-89
Lanza, Black Jack, 117
Larry (see Jack and Larry)
Lasorda, Tom, 124, 127, 130, 133; bottomless jumping-jacking of, 127; naked hockey playing of, 124
Latina butt cleavage, 115
Laura (see Arboleda, Laura)
Lay, Dr., 121-22, 124, 126
Lebanese-American merchants, 35

Led Zeppelin, 90, 130
Led Zeppelin IV, 90
Lee, Thurman, 38, 46
Legion of Super Heroes, the 146
Lex (dorm lothario), 14
Liberace, 23
"Listen to What the Man Says" 61
"Little Darlin'," 113
Loggins, Kenny, 99
London, 47 (see also *quarter abroad in London*)
Lott, Mona, 47
"Loving You," 1
LSD, 46, 95, 150, 151 (see also *mescaline*)
Lyle, Minnesota, 7
Lynn, 71, 79-80
Madison Avenue ("the strip") 36, 37, 113-15, 129, 139
Madison Lake, Minnesota, 26
magic mushrooms, 104
Magnum Force, 59
Magroin, Pat, 48
"Mandy," 36
Mankato Depot, 17-20, 22
Mankato Police Department, 20, 29, 30, 38, 94, 127
Mankato State College (MSC), 7, 37, 41, 53, 55, 120
Mankato State University (MSU), 120, 131, 139
Margaux, 14, 32, 51
marijuana, 3, 11, 15, 23, 25-26, 37, 46, 51-52, 62, 81, 98, 104, 106, 119, 139, 141, 145, 147, 149; decriminalization of, 6 (see also *RoeWeed*™)
Marijuana Mike, 148
Marlboro Man, 4
Marnie, 67-68, 71, 87, 93-94, 97, 105-06, 110-11; jiggly arms of, 68, 93, 105; near-lethal toplessness of, 68-69, 106
Marshall Tucker Band, 138
Marv, 39-41, 42, 75-78, 116; birthday of used as excuse for workplace drug abuse by subordinates, 151; conspiracy against and overthrow of, 95, 97; shameless masturbation in front of female subordinate by, 40-41; tacky Polack jokes and, 75
Mary, Queen of Sots, 2-3, 4, 131-36, 140; latent protuberance of, 132, 133
massage parlors, 28, 67 (see also *Sauna Inn*)
McCartney, Paul (see *Paul McCartney and Wings*)
McDaniel, Wahoo, 7
McElroy Center (residence hall for wayward youths), 13, 21, 46, 144
mechanical bull (as analogue for Ingrid's vagina), 10
Medicine Jug literary magazine, 11
Meldom, Minnesota, 5, 71, 75, 79-83, 92, 110, 120, 128, 132, 134, 141; as cradle of Chest

157

Boxing, 12; as hotbed of well-upholstered cowgirls, 79, 131
Mengele, Josef, 28
Mennonites, 67
Mercury, Freddie, 89
Mercy Rule (in softball), 78, 109
Meredith, Dandy Don, 43
mescaline, 37, 95, 99, 123, 149, 150-53
Mettler's, 32, 58, 59, 60-63, 150; dubious roast beef sandwiches of, 61, 62
Michael's, 144
Michelangelo, 69
Midge, 5
Miller High Life (the champagne of bottled beer), 11, 32, 61, 103, 138, 151
Mindy and Margo, 97-98
Minneapolis-St. Paul, (see *Cities*)
Minnesota River (as analogue for Red's ass), 36
Minnesota Twins, 109
Minnesota Vikings, 1, 4, 5, 91; Super Bowl haplessness of, 1, 4, 5, 91
Minnesota, distinct culture of, 5-8
Missile, the, 18, 27, 29, 31, 37, 38, 69, 79-80, 110, 112, 127, 128, 130, 144, 148, 151, 152-53; cookie tossing of, 79-80; cruising with Arboleda girls in, 112-15; drunk driving on railroad tracks and, 17-20
Moby Dick, 46
Mohicans, 80, 145
Mom (of JM), 93
Mona Lisa, the, 133
Monet, Claude, 153
Mongolian Stomper, the, 117
Monster, Cookie, 91
morality play, 122
Morris Hall, 48
Mortonville Missile, the (see *Missile*)
Mortonville, Illinois, 6, 18
Mother of All Semen Stains, the, 145-47
Motzie, 76-77
Mozart, Wolfgang Amadeus, 89
MSC, MSU, (see *Mankato State College, Mankato State University*)
Nan, 67-68
Napkinland (see *Pearlman Printing*)
Nestlé's Quik, 151
New Ulm, Minnesota, 1
Newton-John, Olivia, 72
Nicholson, Jack, 34
Nicky, 138-40, 142-44, 148
Nielsen, 1-5, 32-34, 44, 47, 54, 58-59, 61-63, 79, 80, 95, 103-04, 105, 110, 120, 128-31, 132-35, 140-41, 148-50, 152 ; as father of Trailer Monstering, 128; Chest Boxing ineptitude of, 12; film criticism of, 103-04, 132; nymphomaniacal girlfriend of, 4, 92; radical orgasm-delaying stratagem of, 93; teenage midlife crisis of, 4; Trans Am of, 4, 128-29
Nixon, Richard, 56, 57
"No More Mr. Nice Guy", 91
North Mankato, Minnesota, 19, 99
Odysseus, 9
Olafson, Kyle, 80
On the Border, 90
one-armed chin-ups (as dance-floor maneuver), 33
"Only Women Bleed", 91, 111
oral sex, 36, 121; implied, 143
Oui magazine, 27
Owatonna, Minnesota, 26
Owl-Man, 13
Pabst Blue Ribbon beer, 25, 109
Pam, 150
Parson Street, 148
Pasek, Chuck, 26; afterlife beliefs of, 53
Paul McCartney and Wings, 61, 106
Paul Revere and the Raiders, 57
Paul the cleaning dude, 35-36
Peace Corps, the, 92
Pearlman Printing, 26, 39-42, 69, 89, 94, 97, 116, 120, 121, 123-24, 125-26, 127, 128, 150-51; softball team of, 74-78, 107-09
Penelope, 9
Penthouse Forum, 1, 5, 123
Phillips, Shawn, 51, 54
Physical Graffiti, 90
Pistol (of *Henry IV*), 74
Pittsburgh Steelers, 5
Plant, Robert, 89
Pluto (quasi-planet), 77, 116
Pollock, Jackson, 35
Pong video game, 131, 133
Posterior Lake, Minnesota, 134, 139
Presley, Elvis, 31
Prodigal Son (see Arboleda Prodigal Son)
Promised Land, the (as represented by Donna James's nether regions), 63
Pryor, Richard, 151
Putski, Ivan, 7
quarter abroad in London, 8, 10, 18-19, 51; obliquely referenced homosexual experience of JM during, 16
Race, Handsome Harley, 7
Rat's, the (see *Rathskeller, the*)
Rathskeller, the, 32-33, 59-60, 62, 63 78, 84, 125, 128-33, 144, 150; demise of, 116; precious-jewel-like qualities of, 59
Reagan, Ronald, 6, 56, 152
recession, 36
Rection, Hugh G., 47
Red, 36-37, 38, 74-78, 102, 107-09; bride of, 108
Reno, Nevada (as locus of senseless shooting

158

death), 35, 36
Reporter, The, 11, 20, 66, 115-16; JM's column in, 20, 32, 39, 51-54, 94, 115 ; possible applications for joint-rolling of, 46
Republicanmobile, the, 7
Republicans, 53
Rita (heroic masseuse), 27-31
Riverfront Drive, 19
Rochester, 25, 29, 31, 116
Roe, Durward, (see *Durward*)
Roe Ranch, 81, 105, 118, 119
RoeWeed™, 119, 147, 151; lack of appeal of, 141
Rome, 42
Romeo and Juliet (as analogues for JM and Rosa Arboleda), 73
Romulus, 42
Ronstadt, Linda, 75, 89, 90
Rosa (see *Arboleda, Rosa*)
Rosencrantz, 91
Rowan and Martin, 57
Sauna Inn, the, 22, 27-31
Sawyer, Tom, 80
Schlitz beer, 60, 61, 74, 77-78, 109; gusto-centric ad campaign of, 75
"School's Out Forever", 91
Shakespeare, William, 74, 95
Shah-Allah-Shah (deliberately misunderstood name of innocuous local band), 114
sheet metal workers, 74-78, 80, 107-09; gusto-grabbing proclivities of, 75 (see also *Red*)
Sistine Chapel, the, 62
skydiving, 24-26, 29, 41, 130
Sleeper Hold, 66
Snow, Phoebe, 138
South Street Saloon, the, 21, 59, 103, 128, 149
speed (see *amphetamines*)
sperm, 13, 21, 22; Canadian equivalency of, 13 (see also *Mother of All Semen Stains*)
Spook (see *Blunt, Stan*)
Spring Street, 50, 65, 69, 86, 111-12, 115, 144
Square Deal, the 59, 129
SS Mayagüez, 55
St. Cloud, Minnesota, 2, 131, 135-36
St. Peter, Minnesota, 41
Stadium Road, 152, 153
Stoltz, Bart (he of the parallelogram-shaped head), 77
Stoltzman Road, 153
Stonebridge, Hedley G., 51-56, 112, 116
Stonehenge (as analogue for Tornado Towers), 98
Stratego, 70
strippers (unacceptable Donna James substitutes), 32, 60 (see also *James, Donna*)
Super America (gas station), 113
Super Bowl, 1, 4-5, 6, 91
Suzanne, Jaclyn, 56

"Sweet Surrender", 150
synecdoche, 46-47, 63
tae kwon do, 45
Tampon Dick (undesirable nickname), 129
taxonomy of inebriation, 84
Ted, (see *Wexler, Ted*)
Ten Years After, 51
term-paper writing business, 20, 51
Tertiary Freddie (see *Freddie*)
Thai stick, 104, 106
"Thank God I'm a Country Boy", 54, 150
THC, 127
Third Avenue (gateway to sinister parallel-universe Mankato), 113-14
Time magazine, 7
Tiny Tim, 11
tits (as adjective), 11, 25, 32, 47, 105, 128, 141, 152; definition of, 128
tits (as body part), 31, 32, 49, 61, 123, 143; of mall manikins, 152; theoretical sweat-excreting property of, 98-99, 103, 143, 149 (see also *breasts, bras, bralessness*) (For that matter, see any old page of this *tour de force* of puerile pap if it's seventh-grade level, elbow-nudging innuendo that you crave. I can't believe I've spent three days of my life doing this. I once published a meticulously researched 120-page dissertation on proto-magical realism in *Mrs. Dalloway*, hailed as groundbreaking by top Woolf scholars, for Christ's sake. Can you *imagine* what it feels like for someone like me to be reduced to compiling an index for the likes of Josh Muggins? Well...no, you can't, can you. You are of the ilk that actually pays money for this filth and reads all the way through the fine type of the Index. May God have mercy on your souls, for I shall have none.)
Tom from Thailand, 133
Tornado Towers, 97-98
Trailer Monsters, 128, 149
trailer park, 112, 115, 119, 123, 134-36, 140, 148-49
Trans Am, (see *Nielsen*)
Trojan War, the, 9
Trojans, stupefyingly lame joke about, 9
trout, sensual flapping mouths of, 124
Trudi, 127
Twin Cities, the, (see *Cities, the*)
Twins, the (see *Minnesota Twins*)
Tyson, Lusty Lonnie, 123-24, 127, 151; penile stitch rupturing potential of, 124
unfuck you curse, 50, 87, 108, 121, 153
Unknown Arboleda Sibling, Tomb of, 85
Vachon, Mad Dog, 6, 7, 66, 124
vagina-obsessed yahoos, 13
Val, 92, 103, 119, 148

Valentine's Day, 21
Valli, Frankie, 72
Velma (shadowy bête noire of Rosa Arboleda), 85, 114-15
Vietnam, 51, 53-54, 89, 114
Vikings, the, (see Minnesota Vikings)
Virgins Anonymous, 45
vodka sour, eyebrow-raising order of, 129-30, 133
Von Raschke, Baron, 7, 65-66; unlikely Omaha roots of, 66
walleye, 29
Wanda, 20-21
Warren Street, 19
Waseca, Minnesota, 26
"Welcome to My Nightmare" tour, 90-91
Wexler, Ted, 89-91, 116; as co-chair of Hate Red Day festivities, 107-09
Wheelbarrow sexual position, 118
Wheeler Park, 74, 127
white cross, (see *amphetamines*)
white slavery, 37
Whooaaaaa! exclamation, 1, 11, 13, 119, 137
Whore of Babylon (see *Kato Ballroom, the*)
Winter, Edgar, 106; as analogue for genital intercourse, 30
wolverine, ferocity of (as analogue for Ingrid's vagina), 33
Wonder, Stevie, 90; greatness of equated with greatness of bralessness, 57
Woodie, 99
Woodstock festival, 56
Woolf, Virginia, (Nowhere to be found, thank God for small favors.)
world literature survey course 117
Writing and Reading the News for Television course, 43-44
Wurlitzer juke boxes, 35, 116
Young Americans, 50
Young, Neil, 36
Yum Yum Inn, the, 20, 35-38, 39, 41, 76, 86, 113; opium-den-suggestive name of, 37
Ziggy Stardust, 90
10cc, 72, 91
2001: A Space Odyssey, 96

NORMANDALE COMMUNITY COLLEGE
LIBRARY
9700 FRANCE AVENUE SOUTH
BLOOMINGTON, MN 55431-4399

9336772R0

Made in the USA
Lexington, KY
18 April 2011